*By fait[illegible] re*
*framed by the w[illegible]*
*things which are seen were not [illegible] of*
*things which are visible*

Hebrews 11:3

*Oswald Chambers' publications*

APPROVED UNTO GOD / FACING REALITY
BAFFLED TO FIGHT BETTER
BIBLICAL PSYCHOLOGY
BRINGING SONS UNTO GLORY /MAKING ALL THINGS NEW
CALLED OF GOD
CHRISTIAN DISCIPLINES
CONFORMED TO HIS IMAGE / SERVANT AS HIS LORD
DAILY THOUGHTS FOR DISCIPLES
DISCIPLES INDEED
GEMS FROM GENESIS
HERE IS GOD'S PLENTY
HE SHALL GLORIFY ME with GOD'S WORKMANSHIP
IF THOU WILT BE PERFECT
IF YOU WILL ASK
LOVE OF GOD
MORAL FOUNDATIONS OF LIFE
MY UTMOST FOR HIS HIGHEST
OUT BRILLIANT HERITAGE
OUR PORTRAIT IN GENESIS
PHILOSOPHY OF SIN
PLACE OF HELP
PRAYER – A HOLY OCCUPATION
PSYCHOLOGY OF REDEMPTION
RUN TODAY'S RACE
SHADE OF HIS HAND
SHADOW OF AN AGONY / HIGHEST GOOD
SO SEND I YOU
STUDIES IN THE SERMON ON THE MOUNT
WORKMEN OF GOD

*Biographies*

ABANDONED TO GOD (McCasland)
OSWALD CHAMBERS (Men of Faith series; Lambert)

# *Gems from Genesis*

OSWALD CHAMBERS

OSWALD CHAMBERS PUBLICATIONS
ASSOCIATION LIMITED

First published as *Our Portrait in Genesis* copyright © 1957 and *Not Knowing Whither* copyright © 1934 by Oswald Chambers Publications Association

Combined edition
first published 1990 by Nova Publishing Ltd
This OCPA Ltd edition 1997



ISBN 1 898009 05 8

Designed and produced by Bookprint Creative Services
P.O. Box 827, BN21 3YJ, England for
OSWALD CHAMBERS PUBLICATIONS ASSOCIATION LTD
22 Sansome Walk, Worcester, WR1 1LN
Printed in Great Britain.

*To our Mother*

whose interest in the sending forth of my husband's messages has been an unfailing source of inspiration.

*—B. C.*

Father, the narrow path
  To that far country show;
And in the steps of Abraham's faith
  Enable me to go.
A cheerful sojourner
  Where'er Thou bidst me roam,
Till, guided by Thy Spirit here,
  I reach my heavenly home.

# CONTENTS

# FOREWORD

*Now these things were our examples* (1 Cor. 10:6).

We know nothing of the beginning of life on this planet earth unless we accept the revealed facts recorded in the Bible. When these early stories are accepted as a true record of individual lives, we can learn much about God's dealings with men and women in every age. There are flashes of light on God's relation to fallen man which can touch a live nerve in a modern wrongdoer, and something of the divine mercy is seen as it persists with perverse and misguided men.

Oswald Chambers brings out the moral significance of human conduct; the intrusion of sin into human affairs, and God's countermove against sin and against the satanic power behind the scenes. 'Now these things were our examples,' wrote the Apostle Paul in reference to some Old Testament incidents. This can be applied to Cain and Abel, to Noah, and to Abraham as we see the subtle working of sin in the unregenerate human heart; of craftiness and insincerity between man and man; of the law of retribution on the one hand, or the due recompense on the other.

Here is a book for today. The Spirit of God is revealing the deep things of God, especially as they bear on the deep things of humanity. Above all, we hear of the God of all grace. 'Who gave his Son to be a propitiation for our sins, and not for ours only, but also for the whole world.'

In this volume are studies of Abraham, that great prince of the life of faith. In him we see faith's reaction to God's call, to clashing circumstances, to the claims of companions, to the terrific cost of God's friendship. These studies link up in a wonderful way the experience of grace under the Old Covenant. Abraham is studied as a forerunner of modern saints in their faith-walk.

This book is replete with spiritual wisdom. The very chapter titles betray that touch of genius, as men call it, which sparkles in the pages. If great books are the life-blood of the world's master spirits, then such a book as this is the life-blood of one who by grace was brought to the fullness of the stature of Christ. These studies make possible a term of guiding reading on this outstanding example of the walk of faith in this world of men.

I thank God for this gallery of portraits in Genesis and for the Spirit's illumination through the expositor's instructed and clear-seeing mind.

*David Lambert*

# FOREWORD
# to the
# NEW EDITION

This volume incorporates the two books by Oswald Chambers, *Our Portrait in Genesis* and *Not Knowing Whither*, with an additional chapter on 'The Tower of Babel', which I have culled from existing O. C. material in my possession. In amalgamating these gems from Genesis in this new edition, our prayer is that these precious truths from the anointed and incisive ministry of Oswald Chambers at the beginning of this century, with its relevant teaching 'in depth', will come with fresh vitality to the church 'in time' for the great spiritual need at the end of the century.

*Arthur Neil*
O.C.P.A.

ONE

# BEGINNINGS

## *Chapters 1–2*

In the beginning God *(1:1).*

I am the Alpha and the Omega, the beginning and the End, says the Lord, who is and who was, and who is to come, the Almighty *(Rev. 1:8).*

THE BIBLE never argues or debates; it states revelation facts, and in order to understand these facts we are dependent entirely, not on intellectual curiosity, but on a relationship of faith. Our perception of Bible truth is of the nature of implicit vision granted by the Holy Spirit, and the remarkable thing about the Holy Spirit's illumination of Bible truth is that it commends itself as being the true interpretation to every child of God who is in the light.

Science (knowledge systematized) is a man's intellectual effort to expound established facts, facts which all intelligent men accept as facts; it is his attempt to arrange these facts into some kind of unity which will not contradict the fundamental way man is made. When we are born again we come in contact with another domain of facts, viz., the Bible domain of revelation facts, and there must be an at-one-ment made between the two domains. Scientific 'truth' is apt to be accepted readily, while we are sceptical over revelations made by the Holy Spirit. Our tendency is to put truth into a dogma; Truth is a Person. *'I am the Truth,'* said Jesus.

> In the beginning God created the heavens and the earth. The earth was without form, and void ['waste and void'] *(1:1–2).*
>
> By faith we understand that the worlds were framed by the word of God, so that the things which are seen were not made of things which are visible *(Heb. 11:3).*

Fundamentally, chaos — the state of matter before it was reduced to order by the Creator — is not to be regarded necessarily as the result of divine judgement, but as the foundation of cosmos, like a painter's palette where he mixes his colours: he sees in it what you cannot. 'Infants and fools shouldn't see half-done work.' We must bear in mind that the constructed world of man we see today is not the created world of God. The basis of man's life has had a formation put upon it which is not of God; what is needed is not the reforming of the basis, but the removal of that which has been erected on the basis. If I build my life on the things which God did not form He will have to destroy them, shake them back into chaos. That is why whenever a man, moral or immoral, sees for the first time the light of God in Jesus Christ it produces conviction of sin, and he cries out, 'Depart from me; for I am a sinful man, O Lord.' When the Holy Spirit comes into a man 'his beauty is consumed away', the perfectly ordered completeness of his whole nature is broken up; then the Holy Spirit, brooding over the chaos that is produced, brings a word of God, and as that word is received and obeyed a new life is formed.

'And the spirit of God was hovering over the face of the waters. And God said, Let there be light: and there was light.' God's word creates, and creates by its own power. God speaks, and His word performs that which He sends it to accomplish (cf. Isaiah 55:11). 'And God saw the light, that it was good.' The matter of God's creation is a satisfaction to God, and when we come to know God by His Spirit we are as delighted with His creation as He is Himself. A child enjoys all that God has created; everything is wonderful to him.

As in the beginning God's word was the creative fiat, and that word's witness to itself satisfied God, so the work of Christ in a disciple witnesses to Him; it is the living Word speaking the words: 'the words that I speak to you are spirit, and they are life.' My value to God is that in obedience to His spoken word I present to Him in actuality His idea in sending it forth; God's word expressed in me becomes its own witness to God. God's word is clear and emphatic, and when we first hear it we are full of joy; then that word has to become its own witness and give Him satisfaction. The fanatic mistakes the vision which the word brings for its expression in actuality. Am I prepared to put God's word into its right place, into the matter of 'me'? If I am, it will bring forth, not my idea, but God's idea, viz., the life according to God. It is not my faith laying hold of the word, but the life in the word laying hold on me, and faith is as natural as breathing, and I say, 'Why, bless God, I *know* that is true!' Strictly speaking, no seed germ contains in itself the maturer growth; it is the other forces acting outside it as well as its own inherent life that determines what it will be ultimately.

> Then God saw everything that he had made, and indeed it was very good. Then God blessed the seventh day, and sanctified it, because in it he rested from all his work which God had created and made *(1:31; 2:3)*.

Six days God laboured, *thinking* creation, until, as He thought, so it was. On the seventh day God rested, not from fatigue, but because that work was finished which enabled Him to rest, immanent in all the laws of nature, in constant manifestation of His overruling power, so that it is as easy for God to perform a miracle today as 'in the beginning'.

> And the Lord God formed man of the dust of the ground *(2:7)*.
>
> The first man was of the earth, made of dust *(1 Cor. 15:47)*.

These verses refer to the fundamental nature of man; don't complicate their meaning by introducing the doctrine of sin at the moment. These two things, dust and Divinity, make up man. That he is made of the dust of the ground is man's glory, not his shame – it is only his shame in so far as he is a sinner, because in it he is to manifest the image of God. We are apt to think because we are 'of the earth, made of dust' that this is our humiliation, but it is not so; it is the very thing God's word makes most of. A doctrine which has insinuated itself right into the heart of Christianity, and has a hold on it like an octopus, is the inveterate belief that sin is in matter, therefore as long as there is any 'matter' about me there must be sin in me. If sin were in matter it would be untrue to say that Jesus Christ was 'without sin' because He took on Him our flesh and blood, 'coming in the likeness of men'. Sin does not belong to human nature as God designed it; it is abnormal. Therefore, to speak of sin being 'eradicated', rooted up, is nonsense; it never was planted in. I have no business to say, 'in Christ I am all right but in myself I am all wrong'; I have to see to it that everything related to my physical life is lived in harmony with and perfect obedience to the life of the Son of God in me.

The Originator and Maintainer of the new life imparted to us by the Redemption is Christ Himself, and our Lord's words in John 6:56 reveal His fathomless conception of that life: 'He who eats my flesh and drinks my blood abides in me, and I in him.' Before, the disposition of self-will ruled—you touch my flesh, and I hit you back; you touch my blood, and it boils in passion. Now, says Jesus, let the very corpuscles of your blood, every nerve and cell of your flesh, exhibit the new life which has been created in you. That life is exhibited in this bodily temple of the Holy Spirit ('or do you not know that your body is the temple of the Holy Spirit who is in you?') it is a fleshly temple, not a spiritual one. The whole meaning of being born again and becoming identified with the death of Christ is that His life might be manifested in our mortal flesh. When we are born from above the life of the Son of God is born in us, and the perfection of that life enables us not only to 'make out' what the will of God is, but to carry out His will in our natural human life.

TWO

# TEMPTATION IN PARADISE

## *Chapter 3*

THERE IS SOMETHING inconceivable to us in Adam's relationship to God. He saw God as simply as we see one another — 'And they heard the sound of the Lord God walking in the garden in the cool of the day' (v. 8). Until Adam fell, he was not *interested in* God, he was *one with* God in communion — a man is never interested in that which he is; when Adam fell, he became so appallingly interested in God that he was afraid of Him — 'and Adam and his wife hid themselves from the presence of the Lord God amongst the trees of the garden.' Sin finds us severed from God and interested only in anything we can be told about Him, consequently there is an element of fear; when we become children of God, there is no fear. As long as a child has not done wrong he enjoys perfect freedom and confidence towards his parents, but let him disobey, and the one he disobeys becomes someone in whom he is interested, with an element of fear. Conscious piety springs from being interested in God — 'I want to know whether I am right with God'; if you are right with God, you are so one with Him that you are unconscious of it; the relationship is deeper than consciousness because you are being disposed by the very nature of God.

When the Apostle Paul talks of a man sinning, *'Therefore, as through one man sin entered into the world'*, remember who it is he refers to, viz., not to a being like you or me, but to the great Federal Head of the human race. Sin is not part of human nature as God designed it; it is extraneous. The Bible looks on sin, not as a disease, but as red-handed rebellion against the domination of the Creator. The essence of sin is — 'I won't allow anybody to "boss" me saving myself', and it may manifest itself in a morally good man as well as in a morally bad man. Sin has not to do with morality or immorality; it has to do with my claim to my right to myself, a deliberate and emphatic independence of God, though I veneer it over with Christian phraseology. If, as a saint, I allow this spirit to get back into me, I become the embodiment of heaven and hell in conflict.

'And the Lord God commanded the man, saying, 'From every tree of the garden you may freely eat; but from the tree of the knowledge of good and evil you shall not eat: *for in the day that you eat the fruit of it you shall surely die*' (2:16, 17). 'And the serpent said to the woman, *'You will not surely die'* (3:4). Eve finds that what Satan told her is true, death does not strike them all at once: but its possibility has come in. Death has secretly begun. We transgress a law of God and expect an experience akin to death, but exactly the opposite happens. We feel enlarged, more broad-minded, more tolerant of evil, but we are more powerless; knowledge which comes from eating of the tree of the knowledge of good and evil, instead of instigating to action, paralyses.

'For the wages of sin is death' — man becomes subject to death, not because he is a finite being, but because of sin. Whenever a man touches sin, death is the inevitable result, it is the way God has constituted him; when he is 'alive' in sin, he is 'dead' to God. 'And you he made alive, who were dead in trespasses and sins' (Eph 2:1). What every human being inherits is not *punishment* for sin but the *disposition* of sin which 'entered into the world through one man, and death through sin; and thus death spread to all men, because all sinned'. Death was not in God's purpose for man. When we are born again we have exactly the experience of going through death. 'You cannot see my face; for no man shall see me and live' (Ex. 33:20) — and yet we do see God and live, but we only see God by going through death. I must die, die right out to my claim to my right to myself, and receive the gift of eternal life, which is 'the gift of God through Jesus Christ our Lord'.

'Then the man said, The woman whom you gave to be with me, she gave me of the tree, and I ate.' Adam does not blame himself; neither does Eve blame herself: 'And the woman said, The serpent deceived me, and I ate.' They both evade the moral truth. Verbal truth is rarely moral truth. It takes a long time to bring me to the place where I will blame myself. Adam *admits*, but there is no confession; he implies, rather, that God is to blame — 'You should not have put me in a position where I could disobey; I don't deny I did wrong, but remember the extenuating circumstances. You shouldn't be so stern and holy.' That is the first manifestation of the spirit of anarchy. The diabolical nature of sin is that it hates God, because when I am face to face with the holiness of God I know there is no escape, consequently there is nothing the natural heart of man hates like a holy God. We don't live deep enough down to realize this. 'If only God would not be so holy as my conscience tells me He is.' It is a mixed-up certainty: I know I am not right with God and I don't want to be — and yet I do. I will do anything rather than take the responsibility on myself for having done wrong; or if I do accept the responsibility, I defy God to readjust me. The one is as bad as the other. I either refuse to say I have sinned, or I admit I have sinned and refuse to let God save me. I won't allow God to have the last word; I have the last word and intend to stick to it. That is the attitude of the devil. 'If we *confess* our sins...' says the Apostle John. Whenever conviction of sin comes, out into the light with it, confess it, because when I realize the shame of it and accept God's forgiveness, there is an inwrought energy brought back in place of the energy which went out in the sin; with the majority of us that energy is lost, it does not come back in 'the fruits of repentance'.

'So the Lord God said to the serpent, I will put enmity between you and the woman, and between your seed and her seed...' (v. 15). God does not deal with Satan direct; man must deal with Satan because man is responsible for his introduction. That is why God became Incarnate. Put it in any other way – why God could banish Satan in two seconds; but it is man who, through the Redemption, is to overcome Satan, and much more than overcome him, he is to do that which will exhibit the perfect fulfilment of this prophecy. Jesus Christ, the last Adam, took on Him our human form, and it is through His seed in that human form that Satan is to be overcome. 'And the God of peace will crush Satan under your feet shortly' (Rom. 16:20). Everything that Satan and sin have marred, God holds in an unimpaired state for every son of man who will come to Him by the way back which Jesus Christ has made.

THREE

# MESSAGE OF GOD ON SIN

## Chapter 4

### Sin Lies At The Door *(v. 7)*

And it came to pass, when they were in the field, that Cain rose against his brother, and killed him *(v. 8)*.

NO MAN can murder his brother who has not first murdered God in himself. Cain's crime is more than murdering his brother; it is a deeper crime within that crime, viz., the putting up of his whole nature against God, and, finally, accusing God for his punishment — 'Of course, my sin is unpardonable if you are a holy God, but you are to blame for being a holy God.'

'So the Lord said to Cain, Why are you angry? and why has your countenance fallen? If you do well, will you not be accepted?' (vv. 6–7). These verses present God doing for Cain what He did for Adam and Eve — giving him a divine opportunity for repentance. Remorse is never repentance; remorse is the rebellion of man's own pride which will not agree with God's judgement on sin but accuses God because He has made His laws too stern and holy. Adam and Eve *acknowledged* their sin although they never *confessed* it. Cain evades acknowledgment; first, he lies to God, then he becomes scornful of God — 'Then the Lord said to Cain, Where is Abel your brother? And he said, I do not know. Am I my brother's keeper?' (v. 9). Sin in Adam and Eve revealed itself as envy of God (see 3:5); in Cain it advances to envy of his brother — 'And the Lord respected Abel and his offering, but he did not respect Cain and his offering. And Cain was very angry, and his countenance fell (vv. 4–5). Personal vindictive rage is the spirit of murder. 'Not as Cain who was of the wicked one and murdered his brother. And why did he murder him? Because his works were evil and his brother's righteous.' 'Whoever hates his brother is a murderer' (1 Jn 3:12, 15).

'And he said, 'What have you done? The voice of your brother's blood cries out to me from the ground' (v. 10). Murder may be done in a hundred and one ways. Think of the number of voices that cry unto God today from men who have been murdered in civilized life. The cry of every murdered innocence, every perverted right, is in the ear of God, and in this sense the blood of Abel still speaks and will never be silenced.

## The Solitariness of Guilt *(vv. 11–15)*

> So now you are cursed from the earth, which has opened its mouth to receive your brother's blood from your hand *(vv. 11, 12)*.

Beware of speaking of *reaction* when God says *retribution*. The man who has done wrong has such a guilty conscience that he imagines everything is against him; everything *is* against him — God is against him, every bit of earth is against him; he stands absolutely alone. Nothing associates itself with the sinner saving his sin. Once sin enters in, you are out of gear with God morally and with the universe physically.

> And Cain said to the Lord, My punishment is greater than I can bear! Surely you have driven me out this day from the face of the ground; I shall be hidden from your face; I shall be a fugitive and a vagabond on the earth... *(vv. 13–14).*

Cain takes God's punishment, which is His mercy, and perverts it into a penal decree making it impossible for him to come back. He entrenches himself in despair as a garment and spits back accusations against God—'See what you have done; I can't get back.' When we are punished by God for wrongdoing our attitude is apt to be—'Oh well, it's no use trying to do any better. God has sent me from His presence, and I can't get back. I can do as I like now.' Beware of making the despairing-sulk complaint, which is found in all of us, a threatening accusation against God. God can never forgive despair. The door is always open to God until I shut it. God never shuts it; I shut it, then I lose the key and say, 'It's all up; whatever I do now God is entirely to blame.'

Look for these things inside yourself; if you don't find them there, you are a humbug to find them outside you. Never disassociate yourself from anything any human being has ever done; that is the delusion of a moral lunatic. God will give you such a knowledge of yourself that you won't be able to say, 'I don't know how anyone could do that'; you will know humiliatingly before God how the vilest crime could be committed. You won't say, 'But I could never do that'; you could. Any human being can do what any human being has ever done. When you see a criminal and feel instantly, 'How horrible and vile that man is', it is a sure sign that the Lord is not in you; if He is in you, you will not only feel how horrible and vile he is, you will say, 'But for God, I am that, and much worse.' But don't use it as a pious phrase; if you don't mean it, never say it.

> Then Cain went out from the presence of the Lord, and dwelt in the land of Nod ['That is Wandering', RV marg.] on the east of Eden *(v. 16).*

Cain had no rest anywhere; the earth spurned him, therefore he went into the land of Wandering and constructed his own world. Men who have sinned and maintain themselves in their sin cannot endure themselves on God's earth, so they must make a world of their own and put it on God's earth. There is no place for sin on God's earth.

> ...and he built a city *(v. 17).*

The first civilization was founded by a murderer, and the whole basis of civilized life is a vast, complicated, more or less gilded-over system of murder. We find it more conducive to human welfare not to murder men outright; we do it by a system of competition. It is ingrained in our thinking that competition and rivalry are essential to the carrying on of civilized life; that is why Jesus Christ's statements seem wild and ridiculous. They are the statements either of a madman or of God Incarnate. To carry out the Sermon on the Mount is frankly impossible to anyone but a fool, and who is the fool? The man who has been born again and who dares to carry out in his individual life the teaching of Jesus. And what will happen? The inevitable result, not the success he would otherwise have. A hard saying, but true.

FOUR

# THE EVOLUTION OF DEPRAVITY

*Chapter 6:1–7*

## THE FLOODS OF ELEMENTAL SIN

> Then the Lord saw that the wickedness of man was great in the earth, and that every intent of the thoughts of his heart was only evil continually *(v. 5).*

DEPRAVITY MUST BE taken to mean much more than going wrong; it means rather to be so established in the wrong that the result is a real pleasure in it. There is an inspiration in choosing to do wrong; it means a simplification of the life. Immediately you choose to do wrong you are not only conscious that you are without excuse, you become brazenly fixed in the wrong; that is the characteristic of the devil. The revelation the Bible makes is not that men are getting worse, but that men are damnable – consequently they are saveable; the system of things he lives in may get worse, but a man can't be worse than damnable. If the mind of man persistently tries to remove the possibility of damnation he destroys the justice of God, destroys his own manhood, and leaves in its place an evolving animal-life to which God is not necessary.

Matthew 15:19: ('For out of the heart proceed evil thoughts....' See also Jeremiah 17:9: 'The heart is deceitful above all things, and desperately wicked;

who can know it?') refers to the depravity of the human heart apart from God. The elemental fountain of depravity is there; the reason it is not manifested to my consciousness is either sheer ignorance by reason of a refusal to accept Jesus Christ's diagnosis, or because I have been saved and sanctified by God's mighty grace. According to our Lord 'these things' are in the mother-heart, that deepest seat of moral character that lies below the conscious, the conscious thought, and still more the conscious purpose. When God's Spirit comes in and opens from underneath our consciousness the abyss we are on, the only thing to do is to completely surrender to Him, and the abyss is closed for ever. It is entire rightness with Jesus Christ alone that prevents elemental depravity working in the heart and out into deeds. If I trust Jesus Christ's diagnosis and hand over the keeping of my heart to Him, I need never know in conscious experience what depravity is, but if I trust in my innocent ignorance I am likely one of these days to turn a corner and find that what He said is true.

When the crisis comes and men find that what they took to be their innocent heart is really a sink of iniquity, they would be the first to say, 'Why did not God tell us?' 'Why were we not warned?' We are warned, perfectly clearly, in order that we need never go through the terrible experience of knowing the truth of what Jesus said – *'For from within, out of the heart of men, evil thoughts proceed...,'* that is the marvellous mercy of God.

Jesus Christ's teaching never beats about the bush. Our stupidity is to believe only what we are conscious of and not the revelation He has made. Instead of its being a sign of good taste, it is a sign of shocking unbelief when men won't face what Jesus Christ has put so plainly, so unmistakably plainly, so brutally plainly at times, about the human heart. Again, let me urge you, never trust your innocent ignorance when Jesus Christ's statements contradict it.

Whenever any choice of ours is based on implicit disregard of God, we are depraved, and this possibility remains in every saint. 'Now I am saved and sanctified all I choose is sure to be right'; not by any means. 'All I think is sure to be right', not so; if our choices and our thinking do not spring from the basis of a determined recognition of God, we are depraved, no matter what our experience spiritually.

## The Foundation of Eternal Salvation

> And the Lord was sorry that he had made man on the earth, and he was grieved in his heart *(v. 6)*.

An unemotional love is inconceivable. Love for the good must involve displeasure and grief for the evil. God is not an almighty sultan reigning aloof, He is right in the throes of life, and it is there that emotion shows itself.

'And it repented the Lord...' (AV). God does not repent like a man, He repents like God, that is, without change of plan or purpose. 'God is not a man that he should lie, nor a son of man that he should repent. Has he said, and will he not do it? Or has he spoken and will he not make it good?' (Num. 23:19). If God were to say of any sin, 'Oh well, he didn't mean it, I will let it go', that would be a change in God's purpose. If God overlooked one sin in me, He would cease to be God. The 'repenting' of God in individual cases means that God remains true to His purpose and must mean my condemnation, and my condemnation causes Him grief and agony. It is not that God won't overlook wrong; it is that He cannot, His very love forbids it. When I am saved by God's almighty grace I realize that I am delivered completely from what He has condemned — and *that* is salvation; I don't palliate it any longer, but agree with God's verdict on it on the cross. At the back of all the condemnation of God put 'Calvary'.

FIVE

# THE CALL OF THE FORLORN HOPE

*Chapter 6:8–22*

## Noah Found Grace

> But Noah found grace in the eyes of the Lord. Noah was a righteous man, and perfect ['blameless' RV marg.] in his generations: Noah walked with God *(vv. 8–9).*

GRACE IS the overflowing immeasurable favour of God. God cannot withhold; the only thing that keeps back His grace and favour is our sin and perversity.—*'Noah walked with God.'* To walk with God means the perpetual realization of the nature of faith, viz., that it must be tried or it is mere fancy; faith untried has no character-value for the individual. There is nothing akin to faith in the natural world. Defiant pluck and courage is not faith. It is the *trial* of faith that is 'much more precious than of gold', and the trial of faith is never without the essentials of temptation. It is to be questioned whether any child of God ever gets through the trial of his faith without at some stage being horror-stricken; what God does comes as a stinging blow, and he feels the suffering is not deserved, yet, like Job, he will neither listen to nor tell lies about God. Spiritual character is only made by standing loyal to God's character no matter what distress the trial of faith brings. The distress and agony the prophets experienced was the agony of believing God when everything that was happening contradicted what they proclaimed Him to be; there was nothing to prove that God was just and true, but everything to prove the opposite. The forlorn hope aspect is the best, perhaps the only idea, for the godly in time: all that has been built up on the basis of personal faith in God is contradicted by the immediate present, and it is the man who does not believe in God who has the safest, best time of it in the immediate present. The Bible is full of this attitude to things (e.g., Psalm 73). It is when we forget this aspect of godliness that we cease to walk with God and only pay court visits to Him; we cease to be His children. To walk with God means walking apart from ultimate godless reliances. There is no such thng as a *venture* of faith, only a determined *walk with God* by faith.

'And Noah begot three sons' (v. 9). Noah's sons are mentioned because in them the continuance of the human race is secure. If you are a snob you won't like the Bible genealogies because they have no respect for the aristocratic notion. Snobbery is the insistence on going far enough back – but not too far!

## My Spirit shall not strive with man for ever

> So God looked upon the earth, and indeed it was corrupt; for all flesh had corrupted their way on the earth... and behold, I will destroy them with the earth *(vv. 11–13).*

It is God's long-suffering patience ultimately coming to the conclusion that He must let the full destruction of His righteousness have its way. 'So God looked' – as if until now God had looked away, giving time through Enoch and Methuselah and Lamech, then suddenly He looks, and destruction swift and almighty comes and there is no reprieve; it means judgement, a final sentence. The pronouncement of coming doom is a combining of judgement and deliverance. When God's limit is reached He destroys the unsaveable and liberates the saveable; consequently judgement days are the great mercy of God because they separate between good and evil, between right and wrong. Salvation to be experimental in me is always a judgement inasmuch as it is concerned with some kind of separation. 'The cross condemns men to salvation.' I remain indifferent to the cross until I realize by the conviction of the Spirit of God that there are certain things in me which are damnable. I can always know the kind of disposition I have got by the sword God brings against me; I may plead and pray, but He is merciless; He saves me 'so as by fire'. When once I am willing to agree with God's condemnation in the cross on those things, God in His infinite mercy, by bringing His judgement, saves. It is not judgement inaugurating salvation, but judgement that *is* salvation. The same with nations, and with the human race.

## Make Yourself an Ark

The ark stands as a reminder that nothing *is* until it is. Whenever we say a thing is impossible the reason is twofold – either our prejudices don't wish it to be, or we say it is too wonderful to be possible. From the building of the ark on, just make quite sure a thing is impossible, and God does it. God can only do the impossible. In the realm of our human possible we don't need God – common sense is our God; we don't pray to God, we pray to an erection of our common sense. It is God who is the Architect of salvation, therefore salvation is not a common-sense design; what we have to do is to get inside that salvation. If I put my faith in any erection of my own, my vows and decisions, my consecration, I am building something for myself; I must co-operate with God in His plan of salvation. Picture Noah sitting down and saying, 'God has given me a wonderful plan. I will watch and see it grow'! *'Thus Noah did: according to all that God commanded him'* (v. 22).

'And behold, I myself am bringing the flood of waters on the earth to destroy from under heaven all flesh...' (v. 17). The initiative springs from the mind of Almighty God, 'And behold I myself am bringing...'; it is not the natural consequence of cause and effect. 'But I will establish my covenant with you' (v. 18), with the new humanity after the Flood. The 'afterwards' of God is never disconnected with the 'before' of His promise, and God's 'afterwards' is more than the fulfilment of His promise; it is the re-expression of the fulfilment of the 'before' of His purpose by my coming into living relationship with Him, if I will.

SIX

# THE DARK OF FAITH

*Chapters 7–9*

> Now the flood was on the earth forty days...and all the high hills under the whole heaven were covered.... Only Noah and those who were with him in the ark remained alive. And the waters prevailed on the earth one hundred and fifty days *(7:17–24)*.

THE ARK itself is submerged, saving the top of it, no foothold anywhere. God removed hope from anywhere but Himself. That is a picture of the kingdom of God in this dispensation: it appears to be completely submerged, yet those very things which look as if they were going to smash it are the things God uses to preserve it.

## THE EXPRESS COVENANT

> But I will establish my covenant with you *(6:18)*.

'Then God remembered Noah' (8:1). This does not mean that God had forgotten Noah; the remembrances of God are sure to those who will put their trust in Him. It is significant to note that whenever the Bible uses terms such as 'repent', 'remember', 'forsake', 'love', in connection with God, their human meaning does not apply, e.g., the love of God can only be illustrated by the character of God.

'At the end of the hundred and fifty days the waters decreased...' (vv. 3–8). The 'at last' of God is never an anticlimax; it always exceeds any possible human forecast. We must be careful never to compromise over any promise of God when by reason of human limitation there has been only a partial fulfilment. Such a compromise is easily detected whenever you feel, 'Oh well, I suppose that is all God meant.' Every word God has spoken will be absolutely fulfilled; to climb down from that confidence is to be disloyal to God. Beware, though, of inferring because no good word of God will fail, that I personally will necessarily partake in its fulfilment; I assuredly will not unless I have come into vital relationship with God by determined faith.

'So he waited yet another seven days' (vv. 10–14). These verses indicate the prominent characteristic of Noah, viz., the humility of patience. Patience is not the same as endurance because the heart of endurance is frequently stoical, whereas the heart of patience is a blazing love that sees intuitively and waits God's time in perfect confidence. It is impossible to be patient and proud because pride weakens into lust, and lust is essentially impatient. Noah stands for all time as the embodiment of the patience of hope.

'Then God spoke to Noah saying, Go out of the ark...so Noah went out... (vv. 15–18). As Noah went into the ark at the command of God, so at the command of God he goes forth of the ark. Had Noah been a fanatic, when God said, 'Go out of the ark', he would have said, 'No, God said "Come into the ark", and this must be the voice of the devil.' There is always the danger of becoming a fanatical adherent to what God has said instead of adhering to God who said it. Noah waited God's time to go out of the ark. The only way to wait for the Second Coming is to watch that you do what you should do so that *when* He comes is a matter of indifference. It is the attitude of a child, certain that God knows what He is about. When the Lord does come it will be as natural as breathing. God never does anything hysterical, and He never produces hysterics.

## The Abiding Relationship

> Then God spoke to Noah and to his sons with him, saying, And as for me, behold I establish my covenant with you and with your descendants after you *(9:8–17)*.

God cannot do certain things without the co-operation of man. We continually ask, 'Why doesn't God do the thing instead of waiting for me?' He cannot. It is the same problem as the difference between God's order and His permissive will. His permissive will allows the devil to do his worst and allows me to sin as I choose, until I choose to resist the devil, quit sinning, and come to God in the right relationship of a covenant with Him through Jesus Christ. It is God's will that human beings should get into moral relationship with Him, and His covenants are for that purpose. 'Why doesn't God save me?' He has saved me, but I have not entered into relationship with Him. 'Why doesn't God do this and that?' He has done it, the point is — will I step into covenant relationship with Him? All the great blessings of God are finished and complete, but they are not mine until I enter into relationship with Him on the basis of His covenant. Salvation is not an edict of God; salvation is something wrought out on the human plane through God becoming Man. Waiting for God is incarnate unbelief; it means I have no faith in Him, I want Him to do something in me that I may trust in that. God won't do it, because that is not the basis of the God-and-man relationship. Man has to go out of himself in his covenant with God as God goes out of Himself in His covenant with man. It is a question of faith in God, the rarest thing; we have faith only in our feelings. I don't believe God unless He will give me something in my hand whereby I may know I have it, then I say, 'Now I believe.' There is no faith there. *'Look to me,* and be saved,' God says (Is. 45:22). When I have really transacted business with God on His covenant and have let go entirely, there is no sense of merit, no human ingredient in it at all, but a complete, overwhelming sense of having been brought into union with God, and the whole thing is transfigured with peace and joy.

SEVEN

# THE TOWER OF BABEL

*Chapter 11:1–9*

## The Origin of Nations and Languages

FOLLOWING THE NEW beginning, after the judgement of the Flood, one language was spoken. This common communication was the bond of their union, the main element of their strength and solidarity. However, they used their unity to nurture and further their own selfish, ambitious desires and plans. The invention of building, instead of being directed by pure motives and the glory of God, was governed by pride in their consolidated determination to build a great city and exalted tower. By their corporate pride they wanted to make a name for themselves. Industry, which is divinely ordained, was motivated by selfish ambition. The disposition of sin deifies self and is geared to the spirit of independence of God and for human gratification. They were also set on contradicting the purpose of God. Their aim was to establish themselves, where they were, contrary to the divine command to replenish the earth (Gen. 8:17; 9:1). 'Come, let us build ourselves a city, and a tower whose top is to heaven; let us make a name for ourselves, lest we be scattered abroad over the face of the whole earth' (v. 4).

Their action was designed to substitute their own plans for God's declared purpose. The 'rebel' is present in the human heart—'my claim to my right to myself'—'I for me'—'we for ourselves'. To oppose the revealed will of God is to court disaster. Pride precedes destruction.

However, God had to act against their human pride, policy and purpose. He made His divine inspection (v. 5), gave His divine indictment (v. 6), took His divine initiative (v. 7) and effected His divine dispersion (v. 8).

> Come, let us go down and there confuse their language, that they may not understand one another's speech. So the Lord scattered them abroad from there over the face of all the earth, and they ceased building the city. Therefore its name is called Babel, because there the Lord confused the language of all the earth; and from there the Lord scattered them abroad over the face of all the earth *(vv. 7–9)*.

The Lord overruled their proud rebellion for His own glory. Although evil may appear to prevail for a time, God's purposes will succeed.

## Solidarity of Sin

*Sin is not in surroundings but in self-interest!* Solidarity means consideration and oneness of interest. The solidarity of the human race—a bastard solidarity—means that every member of the race has one point of interest with every other member. Notice how the whole of Scripture is knit together over this false solidarity of sin. It is quite possible for the human mind to blot God out of its thinking entirely, and to work along the line of the elements which are the same in every man, and to band the whole human race into a solid atheistic community. There are elements in human nature that are the same in everybody, and if once the human mind succeeded in obliterating God, the whole of the human race would become one vast phalanx of atheism.

## Babel of Souls

Here in this chapter (11) we note the first time solidarity was attempted, away back in antiquity. The Bible reveals that there *is* a solidarity of sin, a bond of union, that keeps men together, known as 'the body of sin'; it is the mutual inheritance of the human race (see Romans 5:12). The Bible also reveals that Satan is anxious to keep that solidarity intact as 'the strong man, fully armed guarding his own palace to keep his goods in peace' (cf. Luke 11:21). The body of sin is this tremendous possibility of solid atheism underlying humanity; the share of individual men and women in that body is called 'the old man'. The solidarity of sin forms the basis of the power of Satan, and it runs all through humanity, making it possible for the whole human race to be atheistic. Sin in its beginning is simply being without God. Inevitably this issues in doing without God and acting against God. God's Book reveals the great oracle of evil, the tremendous power behind wrongdoing; it is a supernatural power antagonistic to God (cf. Ephesians 6:12; 1 John 5:19).

When men depart from the Bible they call humanity 'God' in differing terms, the use of the term 'God' means nothing to them. God is simply the name given to the general tendencies which further men's interests. This spirit is honeycombing everything. It is in reality the spirit of the god of this world, the spirit of Antichrist. When we come to the New Testament we find the antidote to all this. By regeneration we are brought into such harmony and union with the God and Father of our Lord Jesus Christ that we realize with great joy that we are meant to serve His interests in His way and for His glory.

## Solidarity of Holiness

In Genesis 11 we read that God caused confusion of tongues; in Acts 2, on the Day of Pentecost, He caused a fusion of understanding by the tongues of fire, the manifestation accompanying the personal advent of the Holy Spirit. The Holy Spirit works in no other way than to glorify Jesus Christ. 'For by one Spirit we were all baptized into one body' (1 Cor. 12:13). Here is the antithesis to the solidarity of sin; it is the solidarity of holiness. The Holy Spirit, by this baptism, delivers us from independent individuality. The one thing He awakens and brings into communion with God is what is meant by personality. Individual self-assertiveness is the husk, personal identity with the Lord Jesus is the kernel. The Holy Spirit builds us into the mystical body of Christ. The body of Christ is an organism, not an organization, and the gifts of the Spirit are not for self-exaltation, but for the good of the whole body of Christ that the Head Himself be glorified.

God is the Architect of the body of Christ, which is composed of those who have experienced regeneration and sanctification, and is the habitation of the Holy Spirit (cf. Ephesians 2:19–22). The baptism with the Holy Spirit is a personal experience which makes individual Christians one in the Lord. The only way saints can meet together as one is through this ministry of the Holy Spirit, not through external organizations. Oh, the foolish fever of these days! Organizing this, organizing that; a fever of intense activity for God. What is wanted is the movement of the Holy Spirit in answer to our Lord's prayer in John 17 — 'that they may be one, as you, Father, are in me, and I in you: that they also may be one in us...' (v. 21). This is 'the unity of the Spirit in the bond of peace' (Eph. 4:3). It is incandescent with the holy glow of the sanctified sobriety of the Lord of glory. There is no danger of confusion where the Holy Spirit, as the unifying Agent, has His right of way in the body of Christ. Remember, when there was the danger of estimating gifts above grace in the church at Corinth, when there was a chaotic Babel of confusion, that great statesman, the Apostle Paul, had to take the matter in hand with his glowing wisdom to reduce it to ordered shape and growth. His sobering word, 'Let all things be done decently and in order' (1 Cor. 14:40) is a salutary warning and corrective still.

Ultimately, 'the meek shall inherit the earth' and then we shall have a system of national life without any of the materialistic crudities seen everywhere today. These are views abroad of a federation of nations and denominations of one kind and another, but it can only come about by the Lord Jesus Christ, by our adherence entirely to Him. Whenever a religious community begins to get organized it ceases to 'draw its breath in the fear of the Lord'; the old way of talking is kept up, but the life is not there, and men who used to be keen on proclaiming 'the gospel' are keen now only on the success of the organization.

However, thank God there is a time coming when this earth will be the habitation of God. At present it is usurped by the world systems of men; when these disappear then God's 'new heaven and new earth' will emerge.

> The holy city, new Jerusalem, will come down out of heaven from God, prepared as a bride adorned for her husband. Behold, the tabernacle of God is with men,

and he will dwell with them, and they shall be his people, and God himself will be with them and be their God *(Rev. 21:2–3)*.

EIGHT

# CROSSING THE BAR

*Chapter 12:1–3*

Sunset and evening star,
  And one clear call for me!
And may there be no moaning of the bar,
  When I put out to sea.

But such a tide as moving seems asleep,
  Too full for sound and foam,
When that which drew from out the boundless deep
  Turns again home.

Twilight and evening bell,
  And after that the dark!
And may there be no sadness of farewell,
  When I embark;

For tho' from out our bourne of Time and Place
  The flood may bear me far,
I hope to see my Pilot face to face
  When I have crost the bar.

*Tennyson*

'NOW THE LORD had said to Abram, Get out of your country....'

'Crossing the bar' is indicative of what happens whenever we act in faith in God. Whatever the faith is in connection with, we have to launch right out on God. To debate with God and trust common sense is moral blasphemy against God. The call of God embarrasses us because of two things — it presents us with sealed orders, and urges us to a vast venture. When God calls us He does not tell us along the line of our natural senses what to expect; God's call is a command that *asks* us. That means there is always a possibility of refusal on our part. Faith never knows where it is being led; it knows and loves the One who is leading. It is a life of *faith*, not of intelligence and reason, but a life of knowing who is making me 'go'.

The personal private life of faith of each one of us has its source and explanation in the life of the Father of the Faithful, Abraham. Abraham's call, with his limitations as well as his obedience, is full of minute instruction with regard to the life of faith.

## The Call of God

The call of God can never be stated explicitly; it is implicit. The call of God is like the call of the sea, or of the mountains; no one hears these calls but the one who has the nature of the sea or of the mountains; and no one hears the call of God who has not the nature of God in him. It cannot be definitely stated what the call of God is to, because it is a call into comradeship with God Himself for His own purposes, and the test of faith is to believe that God knows what He is after. The call of God only becomes clear as we obey, never as we weigh the *pros* and *cons* and try to reason it out. The call is God's idea, not our idea, and only on looking back over the path of obedience do we realize what is the idea of God; God sanctifies memory. When we hear the call of God it is not for us to dispute with God, and arrange to obey Him if He will expound the meaning of His call to us. As long as we insist on having the call expounded to us, we will never obey; but when we obey it is expounded, and in looking back there comes a chuckle of confidence—'He does all things well.' Before us there is nothing, but overhead there is God, and we have to trust Him. If we insist on explanations before we obey, we lie like clogs on God's plan and put ourselves clean athwart His purpose.

> To do our best is one part, but to wash our hands smilingly of the consequences is the next part of any sensible virtue.
>
> *Robert Louis Stevenson*

When Jesus Christ says 'Follow me', He never says to where; the consequences must be left entirely to Him. We come in with our 'buts', and 'supposings', and 'what will happen if I do?' (cf. Luke 9:57–62). We have nothing to do with what will happen if we obey; we have to abandon to God's call in unconditional surrender and smilingly wash our hands of the consequences. Until we get through all the shivering wisdom that will not venture out on God, we will never know all that is involved in the life of faith. Fate means stoical resignation to an unknown force. Faith is not resignation to a power we do not know; faith is committal to One whose character we do know because it has been revealed to us in Jesus Christ. As we live in contact with God, His order comes to us in the haphazard, and we recognize that every detail of our lives is engineered for us by our heavenly Father. If we are going to live a life of faith, we must rest nowhere until we see God and know Him in spite of all apparent contradictions.

> I have to take care not to settle on the sandbank of selfishness, but to leave all for the Lord to order it. If I then make shipwreck, it will be in the wide sea of God's love, the depths of which are as welcome to me

as the surest haven. But nature fights against the thought of venturing forth we know not where, out of self, into unknown regions.

*Tersteegen*

## The Calling of Abraham

Now the Lord has said to Abram, Get out...and he went out, not knowing where he was going.' This is true of a fool or of a faithful soul. One of the hardest lessons to learn is the one brought out by Abraham's obedience to the call of God. He went 'out' of all his own ways of looking at things and became a fool in the eyes of the world. In the beginning faith is always uncertain, because every broad view is at first an uncertain view of particulars. We hear the call of God while we listen to a sermon, or during a time of prayer, and we say – 'Yes, I will give myself to God unreservedly.' Then something happens in our immediate circumstances which does not seem to fit into the vision we have had, and the danger is that we compromise and say we must have been mistaken in the vision. We have to stand true to the fact of God's call and smilingly wash our hands of the consequences. We have nothing to do with the afterwards of obedience. It is easy to want to be always on the mount, but when we come down to the devil-possessed valley we get annoyed or exhausted; we cannot go on with God there. We have perfect faith in God as long as He keeps us on the mount, but not the slightest atom of faith when He takes us into the valley. We have to be careful that the things which are really impertinent actualities do not find us either ignoring them or abandoning our faith in God. We have to go through the trial of our faith in these particulars, because it is the trial of our faith that makes us wealthy towards God.

'And from your kindred....' Personal acquaintance with God shows itself in separation, symbolized by Abraham's physical separation from his country and his kindred. Nowadays it means much more a moral separation from the way those nearest and dearest to us think and look at things, if, that is, they have not a personal relationship with God. Jesus emphasized this (see Luke 14:26). Arguers against obeying the call of God will arise in the shape of country and kindred, and if you listen to them you will soon dull your ears to God's call and become the dullest, most commonplace Christian imaginable, because you have no courage in your faith; you have seen and heard, but have not gone on. If you accept sympathy from those who have not heard the call of God, it will so blunt your own sense of His call that you become useless to Him. Every saint must stand out absolutely alone. Beware lest the sympathy of others competes with God for the throne of your life. Don't look for a comrade other than God when God speaks to you; through *you* will come His purpose.

NINE

# ON WITH GOD

*Chapter 12:4–9*

Not of the sunlight,
Not of the moonlight,
Not of the starlight!
O young Mariner,
Down to the haven,
Call your companions,
Launch your vessel,
And crowd your canvas,
And, ere it vanishes
Over the margin,
After it, follow it,
Follow The Gleam.

*Tennyson*

So Abram departed.

IT IS NOT sin or disobedience only that keeps us from obeying the call of God, but the good, right, natural things that make us hesitate. The natural can only be transformed into the spiritual by obedience, and the beginnings of God's life in a man or woman cut directly across the will of nature. The sword has to go through the natural (cf. Luke 2:35). The call of God comes with a realization that what God says is true, but that does not prevent us from going through the trial of our faith in connection with actual details, and it is when we touch actual details that we begin to dispute with God and say – 'But if I obeyed God here, my sense of justice and right would be injured.' To talk in that way means we do not believe God one atom, although we say we do. The knowledge of God's will is not in the nature of a mathematical problem; as we obey, we make out what is His will, it becomes as clear as daylight. We have to be continually renewed in the spirit of our minds, refusing to be conformed to the spirit of the age in which we live, then we shall 'prove' – literally, make out in obedience – 'what is that good, and acceptable, and perfect will of God.' We have to beware of giving credit to man's wisdom for the way he has taken, when all the time it is the perfect wisdom of God that is manifested through the simple obedience of the man. It is never the acute ability of the saint that is exhibited, but the astute wisdom of God.

## The Concession of Abraham's Faith *(v. 4)*

We must remember that faith in God always demands a concession from us personally. 'So Abram departed', that is, he went on with God as God had commanded him, 'not knowing where he was going.' Watch the debates that go on in our minds when God speaks, whether it is in a big or a little matter. We won't launch out on God's word, we will hug the shore line. 'But it is so unwise to trust God in this matter' – that implies that God has no wisdom at all. If we are going to obey God there must be a concession made on our part; we have deliberately to trust the character of God as it has been revealed to us in the face of all obstacles. 'If God would only come down and explain everything to me, I would have faith in Him,' we say; and yet how little trust we are inclined to have in God, even when we have had an experience of His grace and a revelation of Himself. We sink back to the experience instead of being confident in the God who gave us the experience. Experience is never the ground of our trust; it is the gateway to the One whom we trust. The work of faith is not an explanation to our minds, but a determination on our part to obey God and to make a concession of our faith in His character; immediately we do what God says, we discern what He means. Naturally, man is made to have dominion, therefore he insists on explanations, because everything we can explain we can command. In the spiritual domain nothing is explained until we obey, and then it is not so much an explanation as an instant discernment. 'If any man *will do*...he shall *know*....' If we say 'I want to know why I should do this', it means we have no faith in God, but only sordid confidence in our own wits. 'If God would only give me supernatural touches, I would trust Him.' No, we would idolize ourselves. 'I do not mind being a saint if I can remain natural and be a saint entirely on my own initiative. If I can instruct God about my upbringing and my particular temperament and affinities, and construct my own scenery, then I would like to be a saint.' All along it is the hesitation of the natural refusing to be transformed into the spiritual. In Abraham there was no hesitation, although there were misinterpretations. In the life of our Lord there was no hesitation and no misinterpretations; He combined the great vision of faith with the actual details. The Apostle Paul always applies the great eternal truths to actual details, because that is where faith has to work. The characteristic of Abraham's faith was that he did not select his affinities; he made a concession of his faith to God, and 'went out, not knowing whither he went'.

## The Companions of Abraham's Faith *(v. 5)*

If God has given you a personal revelation of Himself and you have made a distinct concession on your part of faith in His character, you will make a great blunder if you look to see whether others see the same thing. God will undertake to instruct them if you remain faithful to the immediate connections in which He has put you. To live a life alone with God does not mean that we live it apart from everyone else. The connection between godly men and women and those associated with them is continually revealed in the Bible, e.g., 1 Timothy 4:10. If you are going on with God, says Paul, your attitude is to 'labour and suffer reproach' from those who because of apparently accidental relationships go with you, so that by your labour you may bring them to be among the conscious believers. There is a difference between conscious and unconscious salvation. To be consciously saved means that we become of immense practical value to God in this order of things.

## The Consecration of Abraham's Faith *(vv. 6–9)*

Notice the significance of verse 8 — 'there he built an altar to the Lord.' Worship is the tryst of sacramental identification with God, that is, I deliberately give back to God the best He has given me that I may be identified with Him in it. Whenever Abraham neglected to build an altar after God had made a promise to him, he fell into sin. Every act of worship to be effective must be a public testimony to those who in God's providence are with us for worship; it is at once the most public and the most personally sacred act that God demands of His faithful ones. Whenever God has given you a blessing, take time to meditate beside the blessing and offer it back to God in a deliberate ecstasy of worship. God will never allow you to hold a spiritual blessing for yourself; it has to be given back to Him that He may make it a blessing to others. If you hoard it, it will turn to spiritual dry rot. If God has blessed you, erect an altar and give the blessing back to God as a love-gift.

Abraham 'pitched his tent with Bethel on the west and Hai on the east.' Bethel is the symbol of communion with God; Hai is the symbol of the world; Abraham pitched his tent between the two. The measure of the worth of our public activity to God is the private, profound communion we have with Him. Rush is always wrong; there is plenty of time to worship God. There are not three stages – worship, waiting and work; some of us go in jumps like spiritual frogs – we jump from worship to waiting and from waiting to work. God's idea is that the three should go together. They were always together in the life of our Lord; He was unhasting and unresting. It is a discipline; we cannot get there all at once.

TEN

# THE DANCE OF CIRCUMSTANCES

*Chapter 12:10–13*

Not for such hopes and fears
Annulling youth's brief years,
Do I remonstrate: folly wide the mark!
Rather I prize the doubt
Low kinds exist without,
Finished and finite clods, untroubled by a spark.

Then, welcome each rebuff
That turns earth's smoothness rough,
Each sting that bids nor sit nor stand but go!
Be our joy three-parts pain!
Strive, and hold cheap the strain;
Learn, nor account the pang; dare, never grudge the throe!

*Browning*

Now there was a famine in the land *(v. 10)*.

THERE IS A difference between circumstances and environment. We cannot control our circumstances, but we are the deciders of our own environment. Environment is the element in our circumstances which fits the disposition. A man convicted of sin and a man in love may be in the same external circumstances, but the environment of the one is totally different from that of the other. Our environment depends upon our personal reaction to circumstances. 'Circumstances over which I have no control!' is a perfectly true phrase, but it must never be made to mean that we cannot control ourselves in those circumstances. No matter into what perplexing circumstances God's providence may lead us or allow us to go, we have to see to it that in our reaction to those circumstances, which dance around us so perplexingly, we exhibit a personal relationship to the highest we know. It is only by living in the presence of God that we cease to act in an ungodlike manner in perplexing circumstances.

### THE FAMINE IN THE LAND OF PROMISE *(v. 10)*

This must have been a severe test to Abraham's faith. Take it personally; we hear God's word on the mount, but when it comes to the dance of circumstances we are 'knocked out', because we forget that we have to react in those circumstances in accordance with our faith in God. In going down to Egypt, Abraham declined from this standard.

The element of discipline in the life of faith must never be lost sight of, because only by means of the discipline are we taught the difference between the natural interpretation of what we call good and what God means by 'good'. We have to be brought to the place of hearty agreement with God as to what He means by good, and we only reach it by the trial of our faith, never by a stoical effort, such as saying — 'Well, I must make up my mind that this is God's will, and that it is best.'

At times it appears as if God has not only forsaken His word, but has deliberately deceived us. We asked Him for a particular thing, or related ourselves to Him along a certain line, and expected that it would mean the fullness of blessing, and actually it has meant the opposite — upset, trouble and difficulty all around, and we are staggered, until we learn that by this very discipline God is bringing us to the place of entire abandonment to Himself.

Never settle down in the middle of the dance of circumstances and say that you have been mistaken in your natural interpretation of God's promise to you because the immediate aftermath is devastation; say that God did give you the promise, and stick to it, and slowly God will bring you into the perfect, detailed fulfilment of that promise. When and where the fulfilment will take place depends upon God and yourself, but never doubt the absolute fulfilment of God's word, and remember that the beginning of the fulfilment lies in your acquiescence in God's will. Remain true to God, although it means the sword going through the natural, and you will be brought into a supernaturally clear agreement with God. We are not introduced to Christianity by explanations, but we must labour at the exposition of Christianity until we satisfactorily unfold it through God's grace and our own effort.

## The Foreboding on the Line of Peace *(vv. 11–13)*

In the beginning of the life of faith the first element is that of fanaticism. There must be the cutting off, and the maiming, and the separation. There is nothing fascinating about any of that, but when the life has become imbedded in God, and the maiming has disappeared into the full-orbed perfection of a child of God, then that perfection has a tremendous fascination for others even though they do not care anything about God. Then comes the danger of this subterfuge—'I won't tell other people the whole truth, I won't say I am delivered from all sin, or sanctified wholly, that is too rugged, it will offend them; I will cover up the vital testimony and say I am religiously inclined, then I shall be able to preserve my influence with them.' Whenever that cunning rascal 'expediency' comes in, it will bring in its train a foreboding anxiety, which is a sure sign that in that particular we are ceasing to obey God. Our testimony must be unmistakably to the whole of the truth, not to part of it only. It is impossible to go on in our life with God if the element of personal testimony is left out; we will begin to get dexterous with a dexterity that is more or less doubtful, we say the truth but not the whole truth. Whenever God reveals something which we have never seen before and which affects others, a public testimony must be made, and the peril is lest we say — 'But if I stand up and give that testimony, other people will be stumbled.' Whenever we start this doubtful weighing of things we are acting not in accordance with our reliance on God, but in presumptuous confidence that God will see us through if we trust our wits; God will see us through only if we stand steadfastly true to what He has told us. Another danger is to imagine that it is my particular presentation of things that will attract people. It may attract them, but never to God. The line of attraction is always an indication of the goal of the attracted; if you attract by personal impressiveness, the attracted will get no further than you. Our Lord said — 'And I, if I am lifted up from the earth, will draw all people to myself.'

Verse 13 reveals a weakness in Abraham's faith; he does not yet perfectly rely upon the help of God in God's own way and time. This weakness arises from the inability to apply our faith in God to the actual circumstances we are in. We have to be true to God, not true only to our idea of God.

> The failures of the chosen men of God upon a closer examination reveal them as sins of weakness arising from unguarded strength, which failures on the one

hand do not destroy the personal standing with God, but on the other hand render necessary in him a purifying and providential training.

*Foster's Essay on 'The Aversion of Men of Taste to Evangelical Religion.'*

If we imagine we have strength apart from God, we shall have to break the neck of our strength over some obstacle before we are willing to rely upon God. Our own strength is the backbone of the natural life, but if the backbone of the strength of the natural man is removed without planting in the backbone of the life of God, there will be the 'wobble', which persists until the vision of faith and the reality are one and the same.

ELEVEN

# BLANK ASTONISHMENT

*Chapter 12:14–20*

Pure faith indeed — you know not what you ask!
Naked belief in God the Omnipotent,
Omniscient, Omnipresent, sears too much
The sense of conscious creatures to be borne.
It were the seeing him, no flesh shall dare.

No, when the fight begins within himself,
A man's worth something. God stoops o'er his head,
Satan looks up between his feet — both tug —
He's left, himself, i' the middle: the soul wakes
And grows. Prolong that battle through his life!
Never leave growing till the life to come!

*Browning*

WHEN WE SIN directly, we are never blankly astonished at the result. We may be defiant, we may tell lies; or, what is better, we may accept God's forgiveness. Blank astonishment always comes because of failure to do God's will by our very desire to do it. There is no word of censure on Abraham in the Bible for his distinct failure in going down to Egypt on account of the famine in the land God had promised him; but the blank astonishment which it caused is implied all through. Beware of saying what Abraham ought to have done — firstly, because he did not do it; and secondly, because you increase the severity of your own condemnation. This incident is not related for the dishonour of Abraham, but for the honour of God. Abraham did not attempt to vindicate himself.

Beware of thinking (no matter what you say) that God guided you in your decisions; the thought leads to spiritual hypocrisy. God holds His children responsible for the way in which they interpret His will. We only discern God's will by being renewed in the spirit of our minds in every circumstance we are in. We must learn to tell ourselves the truth on the basis of God's word, not on the basis of independent spiritual impulse, although by our blunders of impulse we are chastened as God's sons and daughters.

## The Saint's Guilt in the Wordling's Sin

*(vv. 14–16)*

The result of Abraham's going down to Egypt was perplexity to himself, and he was also responsible for bringing a direct occasion of sin to Pharaoh. Pharaoh treats Abraham with a generosity which must have put Abraham to shame.

Get alarmed when your desire to serve God brings you into such a position that you have to accept, because you cannot refuse, the magnanimous treatment of worldlings who do not know your Lord; because to be in that position means you have transgressed God's order by the very keenness of your desire to do His will; and when you withdraw, as you must do ultimately, it will be with the knowledge that you have been the direct occasion of sin to them.

Christian work is apt to lead individual saints into blank astonishment, because it springs from an eager desire to do God's will. To say – 'I want to do God's will' is to put myself outside God altogether. The striking thing in our Lord's life was that He was not more eager to do the will of His Father than His Father was for Him to do it. He was the Saviour of the world, everything depended upon Him, and yet for thirty years He did nothing wonderful. 'His doing nothing wonderful was in itself a kind of wonder' *(Bonaventura).* Our Lord's life is the exhibition of *the will of God,* not of *doing* the will of God.

Beware in your judgement either on Abraham or on yourself that you do not transfer the judgement to a stage of moral development not yet reached. It is easy to exaggerate. For example, an act that would be criminal in a man is not criminal in a boy. Abraham's transgression must never be classed as a sin morally. He transgressed through eagerness to do the right thing. Transgression is nearly always an unconscious act – there is no conscious determination to do wrong; sin is never an unconscious act. We blunder when we refuse to discern between these two.

## The Saint's Gifts from the Worldling's Sincerity *(v. 16)*

The Egyptian maid Hagar, who became so important an influence in the lives of Abraham and Sarah, was probably amongst the gifts which came to Abraham in Egypt. The friendships and gifts of the world are perfectly sincere, but the saint soon realizes that these friendships and gifts are embarrassing and hindering if he is to remain loyal to God. Then begins the blank astonishment of real perplexity, and God never shields us from anxiety on this score. It is not a case of right and wrong, but of learning through chastening what Abraham learned, that we cannot come eagerly and find out God's will by guessing. We must be renewed in our minds in every circumstance we are in, and beware of suspicions and considerations and suggestions that make themselves seem right to us. Beware of despising the chastening of the Lord, or of fainting when you are rebuked of Him. The only thing to do is to take your blank astonishment, be silent about it, and go on to the next thing.

## The Saint's Groaning and the Worldling's Scorn *(vv. 17–18)*

Pharaoh is a better man than those around him, and he concludes directly that the judgement on his house is from God on account of Sarah, whose person God is guarding as the true mother of Israel. Abraham did not tell a lie, he told a half-truth (see Genesis 20:12).

To say that if a man is committing sin he will hinder the purpose of God, is not true; if a *leader* is trying to serve his own ends, he will hinder the purpose of God. For instance, if I were to try to utilize this house of God for my own ends, the atmosphere of the house would be damaged instantly. Personal sin does not present a barrier in God's house, although it does put a barrier between the one who is sinning and God; but immediately anyone tries to utilize God's house, or God's people, or God's things for his own purposes and ends, then the atmosphere is altered at once. Then the thoughts of many hearts are revealed and there is produced the groaning of the saints and the scorn of the worldling, and the humiliating thing is that in such a case the worldling is right.

## The Saint's Grade in the Worldling's Separation *(vv. 19–20)*

Abraham was dismissed by Pharaoh—a most unspeakable humiliation. If you have made a compromise out of your eagerness to stand for God's honour, you will have to endure to the last limit, as Abraham did, the scorn of the honourable worldling. Instead of your breaking from the world, the world will come with all its courtesy and say — Will you go? By your very desire to stand up loyally for God, you have put yourself in a position where you cannot stand up for Him. The discipline of our lives is to become as little children. A little child would have stayed in the land whether there was a famine or not.

Abraham's going down to Egypt, and his 'dumbfoundering' there, is the reason for all the complexity that came afterwards, and accounts for the continual recurrence of Egypt in the history of the kingdom of God, until at last Egypt is to be united into the great, full purpose of God.

TWELVE

# UNPERPLEXED

## *Chapter 13*

Yea, this in him was the peculiar grace
  (Hearten our chorus!)
That before living he'd learn how to live –
  No end to learning:
Earn the means first – God surely will contrive
  Use for our earning.
Others mistrust and say, 'But time escapes:
  Live now or never!'
He said, 'What's time? Leave Now for dogs and apes!
  Man has Forever'.

*Browning*

...to the place of the altar, which he had made there at first. *(v. 4).*

WHEN WE COME to study the lives of the saints, the confusing thing is that from one standpoint they are a jumble of inconsistencies, whilst from another standpoint they are an exhibition of the boundless consistency of God. This needs to be heeded, because if we study the life of a saint in order to find out what God is like, we shall finish up in the dumps and say – It is enough; whereas if we study God Himself, we shall find that He manifests His amazing consistency in the weakest and feeblest saint. At one time we find Abraham in a blank and sordid muddle; at another, we find him unperplexed and noble. The point is that God remains the same whether Abraham is unperplexed or muddled.

## The Tryst of Sacramental Identification

*(vv. 1–4)*

Abraham went with God, and Lot 'went with Abraham'. Lot went down to Egypt with Abraham, and came back with Abraham, and the abundance of their possessions nearly brought about strife. A life of *faithfulness* is devotion to a servant or handmaid of God; a life of *faith* is devotion to God. Lot continually went to pieces; Abraham never did.

*The Way.* We have to keep tryst with God in contact with the peculiar ways of everyone, and this can only be done by sacramental identification. The one thing our Lord heeded was His tryst with God in connection with everyone, whether it was Judas or Peter or John; He took no account of the evil. We get huffed in no time – 'No, they did not treat me rightly'; 'they did not consider that I ought to have been considered.' Will I keep my tryst with God in contact with the blackguard or the traitor or the saint? Whoever it is, is nothing to do with me. I have not to fit other people into my ideas, but to keep tryst with God in relation to them. I am not to ignore them, but to refuse to look at them from my idea of what they ought to be, and to look at them only as facts in relation to my tryst with God.

*The Wealth.* Abraham came back exceedingly wealthy, but he kept tryst with God over his possessions. Beware of not keeping tryst with God over your possessions, whether they be material or not. It is perilously possible not to, but to make your spiritual life depend on the abundance of things you possess. If God has given you the wealth of divine healing for your body, keep tryst with Him over it. When you are learning to trust God, He gives you at first certain things you lean on; then He withdraws, and you say it is the devil. No, it is the chastening of the Lord because He sees that you are possessing those things. You can only possess your possessions by being detached from them to God who is the Source. If you are drawing your life from God and begin to take a wrong line, God will withdraw His life. This is also true with regard to money. We have only one Source, and that is God. One of the biggest snares is the idea that God is sure to lead us to success.

*The Worship.* All commentators notice one interesting point in Abraham's life, viz. the times he erected an altar and the times he did not; whenever he neglected to erect an altar, he went astray. This fact is one of great significance because worship is the tryst of sacramental identification. In worship I deliberately give back to God the best He has given me that I may be identified with Him in it. If Abraham had erected an altar, he would not have gone down to Egypt, but would have identified himself with God over the famine in the land of promise. Selfishness in spiritual matters produces delusion rapidly. If in every case of blank astonishment, we go back to the place where we first built an altar to God, we will be delivered from the delusion of obtuse independent certainty. Worship is the sacramental element in the saint's life.

### The Test of Self-interest *(vv. 5–13)*

As surely as we begin our life of faith with God, fascinating, luxurious and rich prospects will open to us, which are ours by right, but if we are living the life of faith we will exercise the right to waive our rights and give them away, letting God choose for us. It is the discipline of transforming the natural into the spiritual by obedience to God's voice. In the life of faith God allows us to get into a place of testing where the consideration of our own welfare would be the right and proper thing if we were not living the life of faith; but if we are living the life of faith, we will heartily waive our own rights in favour of those whose right it is not, and leave God to choose for us. Whenever we make 'right' our guidance, we blunt our spiritual insight. The greatest enemy of the life with God is not sin, but the good that is not good enough. It would seem the wisest thing in the world for Abraham to choose; it was his right, and the people round him would consider him a fool for not choosing. Many of us do not go on in our spiritual life because we prefer to choose what is our right instead of relying upon God to choose for us. We have to learn to walk according to the standard that has its eye on God.

*The Tax of Riches* (vv. 5–7). Abraham's riches were in a great measure a tax to him. Every possession is tainted with a want; in this case the want was for sufficient pasturage. When Jesus Christ came He possessed nothing; the only symbol for our Lord is the symbol of poverty (2 Cor. 8:9; Lk. 9:58) and this is true of the saint — having nothing, and yet possessing all things.' Every possession produces an appetite that clings.

*The Touch of Rectitude.* Lot forgot the place of communion; he thought only of the world. But Abraham, unperplexed, instantly exhibited forbearance as the result of his tryst with God; he walked in the moral atmosphere of the Sermon on the Mount. Abraham's rectitude was not the rectitude of honour, but of holiness. This rectitude is exhibited in the life of Jesus Christ, of whom it is recorded that He 'did not please himself'. This gives the deathblow to subjectivity, that is, to the subjective experiences based on what is pleasing to my holy self; of the holiest Being who ever trod this earth it is recorded that He pleased not Himself.

*The Tarnish of Reasonableness* (vv. 10–13). Lot chose what he considered the best for his possessions. This is the tarnish of reasonableness of a mind that has neglected its tryst with God.

## The Type of Supreme Integrity *(vv. 14–18)*

We must distinguish between the times when God revealed Himself to Abraham and the times when He concealed Himself. In the former, Abraham's faith is elevated; in the latter it sinks.

*The Manifestation of God* (v. 14). The first manifestation of God to Abraham was in his migration to Canaan; the first concealing when he went down to Egypt. Abraham did not have another manifestation of God until after his noble act of faith towards Lot.

*The Message of God* (vv. 15–16). The promises of God correspond to the acts and conduct of faith in Abraham. Only when Abraham acts in accordance with his real faith in God, does God speak to him. There is a connection throughout between the providence of God and the conduct of Abraham.

*The Man of God* (v. 18). Paul takes Abraham as a type of the life of faith, not as the type of a saint, but of a tried faith built on a real God. The sanctification of our faith, as distinct from the sanctification of our heart, is the unfathomable, supernatural blessing from God.

THIRTEEN

# WAR

## *Chapter 14:1–16*

Let it go or stay, so I wake to the higher aims
Of a land that has lost for a while her lust of gold,
And love of a peace that was full of wrongs and shames,
Horrible, hateful, monstrous, not to be told;
And hail once more to the banner of battle unroll'd!
Tho' many a light shall darken, and many shall weep
For those that are crush'd in the clash of jarring claims....
Let it flame or fade, and the war roll down like a wind,
We have proved we have hearts in a cause, we are noble still,
And myself have awaked, as it seems, to the better mind;
It is better to fight for the good than to rail at the ill;
I have felt with my native land, I am one with my kind,
I embrace the purpose of God, and the doom assign'd.

*Tennyson*

...and he told Abram the Hebrew...he armed his trained servants *(vv. 13–14).*

In the study of Abraham, as in the study of all Bible characters, principles are no guide. The inconsistencies which we find in Abraham reveal the consistency of God, and the thing to note is that Abraham remained true to God both before and after his lapses. Beware, however, what you call lapses in

Abraham. For instance, there is no lapse on Abraham's part in connection with this war, but rather the presentation of the inspiration of God. Error lies in making the basis of truth an abstraction, or a principle, instead of a personal relationship. Reality is not found in logic; Reality is a Person. *'I am the Truth.'* Spiritual life is based on a personal relationship to Jesus Christ, and on the consequent responsibility of that relationship.

## THE WAR OF VIOLENCE *(vv. 1–8)*

This is the first war mentioned in Scripture, and its cause was the lust for dominion. The war of the world against the world is portrayed in this chapter, and it is full of the most intense spiritual interpretation. Life without conflict is impossible, either in nature or in grace. This is an open fact of life. The basis of physical, mental, moral and spiritual life is antagonism. Physical life is maintained according to the power of fight in the corpuscles of the blood. If I have sufficient vital force within to overcome the forces without, I produce the balance of health. The same is true of mental life. If I want to maintain a clear, vigorous, mental life. I have to fight, and in this way I produce the balance of thought. Morally it is the same. Virtue is the result of fight; I am only virtuous according to the moral stability I have within. If I have sufficient moral fighting capacity, I produce the moral balance of virtue. We make virtue out of necessity, but no one is virtuous who is good because he cannot help it. Virtue is the outcome of conflict. And spiritually it is the same. 'In the world you will have tribulation'; i.e., everything that is not spiritual makes for my undoing; 'but be of good cheer; I have overcome the world.' When once this is understood it is a perfect delight to meet opposition, and as we learn to score off the things that come against us, we produce the balance of holiness. Faith must be tried, and it is the trial of faith that is precious. If you are faint-hearted, it is a sign you won't play the game; you are fit for neither God nor man because you will face nothing.

### The War of Faint-hearted Defence *(vv. 9–12)*

When God's providence involves us unexpectedly in all sorts of complications, the test comes on two lines – will I have faith in God; and will I ally myself with those who rescue the downtrodden irrespective of their beliefs? It is instructive to note in the Bible that faint-heartedness arises whenever self-interest begins to get luxurious. The sign of faint-heartedness in individuals is in the languid talk of 'someone else' when there is anything to be done.

Whenever there is the experience of fag or weariness or degradation, you may be certain you have done one of two things – either you have disregarded a law of nature, or you have deliberately got out of touch with God. There is no such thing as weariness in God's work. If you are in tune with the joy of God, the more you spend out in God's service, the more the recuperation goes on, and when once the warning note of weariness is given, it is a sign that something has gone wrong. If only we would heed the warning, we would find it is God's wonderfully gentle way of saying – 'Not that way; that must be left alone; this must be given up.' Spiritual fatigue comes from the unconscious frittering away of God's time. When you feel weary or are exhausted, don't ask for hot milk, but get back to God. The secret of weariness and nervous disease in the natural world is the lack of a dominating interest, and the same is true in spiritual life.

Much of what is called Christian work is veneered spiritual disease; it is Christian activity that counts — dominating life from God, and every moment is filled with an energy that is not our own, a superabounding life that nothing can stand before.

## THE WAR OF DIVINE INSPIRATION *(vv. 13–16)*

In chapter 13 Abraham was put through the test of self-interest, and here he is put through the test of self-complacency. The occasion for self-complacency would be in seeing that what befell Lot was just, and that God was proving Abraham to be in the right. But Abraham did not go under in the test; he did not sit down, as it were, with a sanctified smirk and say, 'Perhaps he will learn wisdom now.' Abraham entered into the war with the light and cheerful heroism of heaven.

'...servants, born in his own house.' This phrase is of great spiritual significance. When a conflict takes place, such as is pictured here, the successful fighters are the faithful children of the faithful saints. In spiritual warfare may God have mercy on the barren saint who has never produced his own kind but has to rely upon the converts of others. In the rugged details of the Old Testament regarding marriage, there is always a spiritual revelation. In the natural world there are three — father, mother and child; and in the spiritual world there are three — God, church and converts. If a spiritual nature cannot reproduce its own kind, it will have to answer to God for it. If you have to rely in times of stress upon the converts of others, the conflict drags out desperately; you can always rely on your own converts, those whom you have been the means of leading into the truth.

FOURTEEN

# MORE THAN CONQUEROR

*Chapter 14:17–24*

Why have we yet no great deliverance wrought,
Why have we not truth's banner yet unfurled,
High floating in the face of all the world,—
Why do we live and yet accomplish nought?
What time the years pass from us of our youth,
And we unto the altar of high truth
As yet no worthy offering have brought.
But now we bid these restless longings cease;
If Heaven has aught for us to do or say,
Our time will come; and we may well hold peace,
When He, till thrice ten years had passed away,
In stillness and in quietness upgrew,
Whose word once spoken should make all things new.

*Trench*

Now consider how great this man was, to whom even the patriarch Abraham gave a tenth of his spoils *(Heb. 7:4).*

WE HAVE to live perfectly actual lives, not actually perfect lives. This fact makes all the difference between religious faith and religious farce, and is very clearly brought out in the life of Abraham. God is not actual, He is real, and He bears into me His Holy Spirit who enables me to live a perfectly actual life, kept by the reality of the love of God. 'I don't feel this and that'—how can you when God is not actual, but real? Feeling has to do with actualities and will come later. Right feeling is produced by obedience, never vice versa. I am brought into contact with actuality by my senses, and into contact with reality by my faith. The test in actual things is – am I living a life of faith, or a life of common sense which denies faith? Faith does not make me *actually perfect*; faith makes me *perfectly actual*.

### When the Victory is Won *(v. 17)*

The supreme test in the perfectly actual life of faith comes after a victory has been gained, because in the expansive hour of relaxation the ruling disposition of the heart is instantly manifested. We read of our Lord that after a day when 'all the city was gathered together at the door', He rose up a great while before day in order to pray, not to praise (Mk 1:32–35). In Abraham the victory revealed that he was more than conqueror over himself. To say 'I have got the victory' is a selfish testimony; the testimony of the Spirit of God is that the Victor has got me. If we can notify victories for ourselves, we are not in right relationship to God at that particular time. Instead of worshipping God we are conscious only of what He has done through us, and we triumph in the experience He has brought us. My actual life is given me by God, and I can live in it either as an atheist or as a worshipper. Abraham stands as one who worships God after a victory.

### Where the Victor is a Worshipper *(vv. 18–20)*

Just where Abram stands as the most striking character, Melchizedek enters and towers above him.

What better type or symbol could there be of the

> absolute, the everlasting, because the divine, high priesthood and kingship than that phenomenal figure of Melchizedek? He comes out of the invisible, timeless eternity of the past; he belongs to the timeless assured eternity of the future; he is High Priest forever.
>
> *Du Bose*

Melchizedek is a type of Christ; Abraham is never taken as a type of Christ, he is a type of the perfectly actual children of God. Melchizedek represents the Incarnation of God; Abraham represents the life of faith in the God who became Incarnate. 'Christ in me' and 'I in Christ'; 'Christ the Lord' and 'Christ the Servant' — all become simple when we understand the relationship of Melchizedek and Abraham.

The supreme lesson of the perfectly actual life of faith is to learn how to worship. Faith brings me into personal contact with God before whom I must ever bow. I have to maintain a worshipful relationship to God in everything, and in the beginning this is difficult. I am all right at meetings, at anything that is illuminated, but when it comes to actual life, I am actually of no use. I can talk till further orders, but don't ask me to live the life.

We have to contend for God in our actual circumstances, and our contention for God lies in seeing that we rely upon Him absolutely while we carry out the dictates of our faith in Him. Melchizedek brings bread and wine to refresh the heroes of the perfectly actual life. Christ never takes part in the perfectly actual mix-up of our human lives; therefore to ask 'What would Jesus do?' is not the question of faith, but of Pharisaism. The question to ask is — *'What would Jesus have me do?'* It is impossible for Christ to be where you are, that is why he has put you there. You have to put on the new man in the actual circumstances you are in and manifest Him. It is arrogant humbug to imagine we are to be God Almighty on this earth. We are to be the sons and daughters of God, to live actual lives and put on the new man by deliberate acts of faith all the time, not denying the actual life. We have to remember that our bodies are the temples of the Holy Ghost, and to see that God is manifested in our mortal flesh by our worship; and that can only be done as we take the nourishment, the bread and the wine, which will sustain us in our actual contentions for God. 'For in that he himself has suffered, being tempted, he is able to aid those who are tempted,' i.e., succour us with His bread and wine in the hour of our temptation (Heb. 2:18; 4:15).

It is dangerous to take Abraham as the picture of sanctification. Sanctification means the perfection of Jesus Christ manifesting itself in actual experience. If you take Abraham as a picture of sanctification, you will have to chop his life up and say—This part is sanctification, and that is not; and you will produce a false spiritual interpretation. Abraham is a picture of the life of faith, not the result of faith. He portrays for all time the ups and downs, the haphazards and the tests, the nobilities and the blunders of the perfectly actual life of faith.

## While the Victorious is Worthy *(vv. 21–24)*

Abraham renounces any advantage for himself, but he preserves the rights of those with him. We have the perfect right not to insist on our rights—it is the privilege of a Christian to waive his rights; but we do not always recognize that we must insist on those associated with us getting their rights. If they prefer to take the line of faith that we take, that is their responsibility, but we are not exonerated from seeing that they get their rights.

FIFTEEN

# A STAR HITCHED WAGON

## *Chapter 15:1–6*

Be near me when my light is low,
  When the blood creeps, and the nerves prick
  And tingle; and the heart is sick,
And all the wheels of Being slow.

Be near me when the sensuous frame
  Is rack'd with pangs that conquer trust;
  And Time, a maniac scattering dust,
And Life, a Fury slinging flame.

*Tennyson*

And he believed in the Lord *(v. 6)*.

THE TITLE represents the wildness of God's expectations. If only He had told us to hitch our wagon to a mule, we could see how it might be done; but to tell us to hitch our natural lumbering wagons to the star of Almighty God makes us wonder whether we have understood Him aright. Faith sticks to the wagon and the star; fanaticism jumps from the wagon to the star and breaks its neck. A saint is not an angel and never will be; a saint is the flesh and blood theatre in which the decrees of God are carried to successful issues. All of which means that God demands of us the doing of common things while we abide in Him.

## The Vision in the Valley of Afterwards *(v. 1)*

The meaning of the valley of afterwards is that there must be an interchange between actualities and realities; it is the successful interchange between the two that keeps the life healthy. There is no 'afterwards' to the one who lives his life mystically only; a life that produces no results is an intensely selfish life. There must be the interchange between my real standing before God and my life on the earth, i.e., my wagon must be hitched to the star, and hitched to it by faith.

The afterwards of success for God produces the feeling – Was it worthwhile? The coward fears before danger; the heroic spirit fears afterwards. It was after the victory, when Abraham went into the valley of the afterwards, that God said to him – 'Do not be afraid Abram, I am your shield, your exceedingly great reward.' If you say, 'My goal is God Himself' before you have been to school, it is merely a nursery rhyme; but say it after winning a victory that tells for God, and the victory does not seem such a glorious thing after all, until you find that the goal is not a prize, but the fulfilment of a decree of God in and through you.

## The Veil on the Vision of Abraham *(vv. 2–3)*

Abraham is not rebellious, but he is not hilarious. He believes that Eliezer must be his heir, and he acquiesces in the purpose of God and only wants light as to the meaning of it. The phrase – 'Look, you have given me no offspring' is not a murmur against God, but a pious exclamation of weakness. It is not a challenge to God, but an expression of resignation; Abraham is blaming himself for misinterpreting God – 'Excuse me for being so disappointed, Lord, but I find that all my hopes and ideas have been wrong'; but he came to find that they were not wrong.

Beware of being sorry for God's reputation in your particular case. Self-pity is satanic; but pity for God is the betrayal of your affections. Here Abraham is in the condition not of pitying himself, but of pitying God's reputation in himself; he cannot understand how God is going to fulfil what He has said – no heir other than Eliezer, the idea of having a child must have been a misinterpretation. The veil on the vision of Abraham makes him say: It can't be done – I want an explanation as to your meaning. When God's promise refers to fertility in mud, we must not think it refers to birds of paradise in heaven, and because we see the mud only and no sign of fertility, say we are mistaken. If any promise of God that has emphatically to do with this earth and with flesh-and-blood people is not being fulfilled, beware of saying – Oh well, I must have misinterpreted what God meant. We forget that we have to build in absolute confidence on God. There is nothing more heroic than to have faith in God when you can see so many better things in which to have faith. It is comparatively easy to have faith in God in a pathetic way in the starvation of things round about you, but a different matter to have faith in God after a tremendous victory has been won, and then in the aftermath that follows to think that there is to be no realization of that for which God has caused you to hope.

### The Voice and the Vastness of Altitude *(vv. 4–5)*

In this chapter we fathom the depths of all that the New Testament unfolds. Abraham the childless is to become the father of nations – how mad the promise sounds! 'Then he brought him outside and said, Look now toward heaven, and count the stars...So shall your descendants be.' God points Abraham away from his wagon in the mud to the starry night, and hitches the two together by His own word. God's appeal to the stars is not to furnish proof for a doubting mind, but to provide nourishment for a faltering faith. Nature to the saint is a sacrament of God, not merely a series of facts; not symbols and signs, but the real evidence of the coming of God as a sacrament to His faithful children.

The whole discipline of the life of faith is to mix together the light of heaven and the sordid actuality of earth. Contemplation and consideration must go together, i.e., take your plan for what you do on earth from the altitude of heaven; let contemplation of the stars be mixed with what you build on earth.

In personal life despise these two things — dumps and hurry; they are worse than the devil, and are both excessively culpable. Dumps is an absolute slur against God — I won't look up, I have done all I could but it is all up, and I am in despair. Hurry is the same mood expressed in an opposite way — I have no time to pray, no time to look to God or to consider anything, I must do the thing. Perspiration is mistaken for inspiration. Consequently I drive my miserable little wagon in a rut instead of hitching it to a star and pulling according to God's plan. God hitched the wagon of Abraham to the stars which He had created, by His word. In our personal lives the great solution is always found in the words of our Lord when we have His Spirit. Jesus Christ is God Incarnate, and He makes His words spirit and life to us; our little human wagons are hitched to the star of God's sacramental purpose by the words of Jesus and in no other way. Whenever we indulge in hurry or in the dumps and refuse to pay attention to His words, we smash the connecting line and go off on our own.

### The Veracity and Virtue of Attitude *(v. 6)*

'And he believed in the Lord.' This is the act by which Abraham goes out of himself and relies upon God for righteousness and grace. Abraham had manifested many noble qualities of heart and many virtues in his walk of faith, but he is not made righteous before God by these. The lack in Abraham is supplied through his living confidence in God. The justification of every sinner is by faith and by faith alone, and when a man walks in that faith his justification appears in his flesh and justifies God (see Psalm 51:4).

This verse is the first germ of the great doctrine of 'The Lord our Righteousness'. Righteousness must never be made to mean less than a guiltless position in the presence of justice and right. God justifies me by my supernatural faith in Him, but it is my just walk that proves Him just in saving me; if I do not walk in the life of faith, I am a slander to God.

SIXTEEN

# GOOD *VERSUS* BEST

*Chapter 16:1–6*

How the world is made for each of us!
  How all we perceive and know in it
Tends to some moment's product thus,
  When a soul declares itself — to wit,
By its fruit, the thing it does!

Be hate that fruit or love that fruit,
  It forwards the general deed of man.
And each of the Many helps to recruit
  The life of the race by a general plan;
Each living his own, to boot.

*Browning*

She fled from her presence *(v.6)*.

IN THE SPIRITUAL life we do not go from good to better, and from better to best; because there is only One to whom we go, and that One is the Best, viz., God Himself. There can be no such thing as God's second best. We can perversely put ourselves out of God's order into His permissive will, but that is a different matter. In seeking the Best we soon find that our enemy is our good things, not our bad. The things that keep us back from God's best are not sin and imperfection, but the things that are right and good and noble from the natural standpoint. To discern that the natural virtues antagonize surrender to God is to bring our soul at once into the centre of our greatest battlefield. Very few of us debate with the sordid and the wrong, but we do debate with the good; and the higher up we go in the scale of the natural virtues, the more intense is the opposition to Jesus Christ, which is in inverse ratio to what one would naturally imagine (cf. Matthew 23:31).

### The Fanaticism of Self-denial *(vv. 1–2)*

The childless state of Abraham's house was its great sorrow, and was a constant trial to Abraham's faith. Everything to do with Abraham's call was dependent upon his having seed. It is instructive to note where both Abraham and Sarah began to go wrong. They did their best to fulfil God's command, but in so doing they got out of God's order into His permissive will. The fanatical passionate desire to fulfil God's will led them into desperate error. Beware of the fanaticism of self-denial; it will lead to error lasting in its effects. When we go off on that line we become devoted to our interpretation of our destiny. Destiny is never abstract. The destiny of a human being is vested in personal relationship to God. Abraham learned this lesson later; on Mount Moriah he distinctly proved that he knew the difference between obeying what God said and obeying God who said it. Fanaticism is sticking true to my interpretation of my destiny instead of waiting for God to make it clear. The fanatical line is — *Do* something; the test of faith lies in *not* doing. Fanaticism is always based on the highest I believe; a sordid being is never fanatical. Our Lord taught His disciples to pray — 'Do not lead us into temptation.' To say — 'Lord, I will do whatever you tell me to do; I will stand loyal to you' is deliberately to disobey this caution of our Lord.

Natural impulse in a saint leads to perdition every

time unless it is brought into obedience to the destiny of God; then it is turned into inspiration. It is not that impulse is wrong, but it will lead to wrong unless it is brought into obedience to the spiritual destiny of the life, and this can only be done by devotion to the One who founds our destiny for us, our Lord Himself. Beware of trying to forestall God's programme by your own impulse.

### The Falsity of Sagacious Discernment *(v. 4)*

Abraham and Sarah both adhered to their sagacious discernment in acting in accordance with the practice of the time in which they lived. Beware of discerning according to your own sagacity how God must do some things, because it means that you dictate to God — That word of God must be fulfilled; I cannot allow that I have been deluded, therefore there is only one thing left to do. That is leaning to your own understanding instead of trusting in the Lord with all your heart. Never say — God must do this thing. He must not; God will fulfil His own word. You have no business to dictate to Him; you have to remain true to God and when His word is fulfilled, you will know He has fulfilled it because it is a supernatural fulfilment. Always beware of being more eager to do God's will than God is for you to do it. The remarkable thing about the life of our Lord was not that He was eager to do God's will, but that He was *obedient* to do it. He never put His fingers across the threads of His Father's providential order for Him and gave a tug saying — 'Now I will help you,' and pulled the thing right out of His Father's hands. He simply obeyed, leaving His Father's wisdom to arrange all for Him. We rush in and say — I see what God wants and I will do it, and we wound our own souls and injure other lives.

## The Frenzy of Spent Devotion *(v. 5)*

Sarah's appeal in which she demands that the wrong should be upon Abraham—'My wrong be upon you'—is a passionate outbreak. The whole thing is the consequence of the wrong into which Abraham has allowed himself to be drawn. It is significant to note that both Adam and Abraham receive the severe judgement of God; they heeded the voice of their wives and they had no business to. The full force of God's judgement comes on the man, not on the woman. All through it is man who is held responsible; he may escape from man's judgement but never from God's judgement ultimately. Nothing in the way of judgement is visited by God on the woman (cf. 1 Timothy 2:14); in human judgement it is the opposite. In this case the punishment fell distinctly on Abraham, although the instigation came from the fanatical self-denial of Sarah. God never holds a woman responsible in the same way as He does a man.

## The Fanaticism of Sensual Dominion *(v. 6)*

Sarah through her harsh treatment of Hagar evidently thrust her back into the position of a mere slave; Hagar believed that she had grown above that position, and fled. Hagar does not stand for sin, but for the natural life when it gets out of place and up against the spiritual life. Hagar and her son received real protection and blessing from God. Sin can never be in a subordinate position. My natural life must be in subordination and under the absolute control of the spiritual. The natural must be turned into the spiritual by obedience, whatever sword has to go through its heart. The natural life must be 'spiked' for the glory of God. The characteristic of the natural life is the independent passion for free dominion over itself.

Immediately the natural life fights to get away, it comes into opposition. It is the *good* that hates the *best*. It is not only sin that produces the havoc in life, but the natural determination to 'boss the show' for God and everyone else.

SEVENTEEN

# CONTINUOUS CONVERSION

*Chapter 16:7–16*

Lord, I have fallen again — a human clod!
Selfish I was, and heedless to offend;
Stood on my rights. Thy own child would not send
Away his shreds of nothing for the whole God!
Wretched, to thee who savest, low I bend:
Give me the power to let my rag-rights go
In the great wind that from thy gulf doth blow.

Keep me from wrath, let it seem ever so right:
My wrath will never work thy righteousness.
Up, up the hill, to the whiter than snow-shine,
Help me to climb, and dwell in pardon's light.
I must be pure as thou, or ever less
Than thy design of me — therefore incline
My heart to take men's wrongs as thou tak'st mine.

*George MacDonald*

Where have you come from?...Return...and submit *(vv. 8–9).*

HAGAR REPRESENTS the natural life; she does not represent sin — sin cannot be converted. I have continually to convert the natural life into submission to the Spirit of God in me and not say — I will never do anything natural again; that is fanatical. When by the providence of God my body is brought into new conditions, I have to see that my natural life is converted to the dictates of the Spirit of God in me. Because it has been done once is no proof that it will be done again. 'Unless you are converted, and become as little children...' is true for all the days of the saintly life; we have continually to turn to God. The attitude of continuous conversion is the only right attitude towards the natural life, and it is the one thing we object to. Either we say the natural is wrong and try to kill it, or else we say that the natural is all there is, and that everything natural and impulsive is right. Neither attitude is right. The hindrance in spiritual life is that we will not be continuously converted; there are 'wadges' of obstinacy where our pride spits at the throne of God and says — 'I shan't; I am going to be boss.' We cannot remain boss by the sheer power of will; sooner or later our wills must yield allegiance to some force greater than their own, either God or the devil.

## THE ANGEL OF THE LORD AND WRECKED PASSION

*(v. 7)*

Hagar in her helpless condition is in a fit state for the angel of the Lord to appear to her. Sarah's fanatical self-denial and vindictive spite are far from right, but they do not justify Hagar for her passionateness. I alone am responsible for the wrong I do. Hagar desired to be the mother of the seed of Abraham, but she was not to be; in her own mind she insisted on being not only the equal of Sarah but her displacer. Beware of passion that makes you reach for position, because it will end in spiritual infamy. Passion is the combination of desire and pride with a wild reach of possibility. The desire may be for a big or a little thing, but the instant result of anything done at the spur of passion lands you in a wilderness of disgust, nursing wounded pride.

The right relationship of Hagar to Sarah is to be the

relationship of my natural life to the domination of the Holy Spirit. My natural life must not rule; the spiritual must rule, and it must rule over the natural life, which is represented by Hagar. I have to convert my natural life continually into submission to the Spirit of God in me, otherwise I shall produce the divorce which ends in hell.

## The Angel of the Lord and Wounded Pride
*(vv. 8–9)*

The angel of the Lord and conscience say the same thing — Return and submit — yet they stand distinct. If the voice of God does not correspond with what conscience says, I need pay no attention to it; but when it says the same thing as conscience, I must either obey or be damned in that particular. Return from assumed responsibility and submit — to the old oppression? Yes, but without the element of passion and of pride, and the result will be according to the will of God.

Natural pride has to do with my standing before men, not before God — I shall not bow, I will make others bow to me. That is natural domination, and represents the antagonism of the natural life to the domination of the Holy Spirit. Wherever there is natural pride the Lord must inevitably be put to open shame.

## The Angel of the Lord and the Word of Promise *(vv. 10–12)*

'The Lord has heard your affliction.' Throughout the Bible this is the revelation of the personal attitude of God to the miseries of the world. He is not indifferent, the cry does not go up to the ears of a deaf God.

Hagar's great desire is to be the mother of the

believing children of Abraham; the angel says — No, Hagar is to be the mother of Ishmael, and Ishamel is to be blessed. The limitation of the promise is connected with the promise itself. Do not miss the point of Hagar's mistake. Hagar must be cured of the delusion that she is destined to become the mother of the believing seed of Abraham — 'Cast out the bondwoman and her son'; i.e. cast them out of the position they have no right to be in (see Galatians 4:30).

The attitude of our Lord towards anything to do with the natural is that of unflinching, patient sternness; He is not cruel, but He is stern, just as He was stern with His mother (Jn 2:4), and just as the Apostle Paul was stern with his own body (1 Cor. 9:27).

When we are born again we enthrone Ishmael, that is, we consecrate our natural gifts and say these are the things with which God is going to do His work; they are the things God makes His servants, and I have to see that they are put in the position of servants. If I put them on the throne, I start a mutiny within my own soul. The bondwoman and her child have to be cast out; the natural has to be sacrificed in order that it may be brought into perfect at-home-ness with the Spirit of God. If we make our natural life submit and obey the Holy Spirit within us, we will hasten the time for the manifestation of the sons of God (Rom. 8:21). It is the man who can rule his natural spirit that is able to take the city. It is only when we have learned to bring the natural life into perfect submission to the ruling personality of God that God dare turn His saints loose. It is of no use to turn out a lot of 'half-baked Ephraims' into unlimited power. If I enthrone natural pride or natural virtue, I am in total insubordination to God in just that particular and cannot be His son or daughter.

## The Appearing of the Lord and Waiting Patience *(vv. 13–16)*

'You-Are-the-God-Who-Sees.' We *see* for the first time when we do not look. We see actual things, and we say that we see them, but we never really see them until we see God; when we see God, everything becomes different. It is not the external things that are different, but a different disposition looks through the same eyes as the result of the internal surgery that has taken place. We see God, and then we see things actually as we never saw them before.

EIGHTEEN

# THE RESERVATIONS OF GOD

*Chapter 17:1*

Oh, we're sunk enough here, God knows!
  But not quite so sunk that moments,
Sure tho' seldom, are denied us,
  When the spirit's true endowments
Stand out plainly from its false ones,
  And apprise it if pursuing
Or the right way — or the wrong way,
  To its triumph or undoing:

There are flashes struck from midnights,
  There are fire-flames noondays kindle,
Whereby piled-up honours perish,
  Whereby swollen ambitions dwindle,
While just this or that poor impulse,
  Which for once had play unstifled,
Seems the sole work of a life-time
  That away the rest have trifled.

*Browning*

I am the Almighty God *(v. 1).*

GOD IS A perplexing Being to man because He is never in the wrong, and through the process of allowing every bit of man's wrongdoing to appear right at the time, He proves Himself right ultimately. Beware of the conception that God has to use His wits to keep Himself from being outwitted by man and the devil. God will never have more power than He has now; if He could have, He would cease to be God. Individually we may thwart God's purpose in our lives for a time, but God's purpose will be fulfilled, wherever we end. Human free will is God's sovereign work, and God not only respects it in man but He delights to posit it in him. I have perfect power not to do God's will, and I have that power by the sovereign will of God; but I can never thwart God's will ultimately. God allows ample room for man and the devil to do their worst; He allows the combination of other wills to work out to the last lap of exhaustion so that that way need never be tried again, and men will have to confess, either reluctantly or willingly, that God's purpose was right after all. And this holds true in the individual lives of God's children. I am at liberty if I choose to try every independent plan of my own, but I shall find in the end (whether too late or not is another matter), that what God said I had better do at the beginning was the right thing, if only I had listened to Him.

Every blunder Abraham made was repeated in his descendants by the inevitableness of God's providence. The consequence of doing wrong is brought out in the life of Abraham in great prominence, but the abiding truth remains the same for each one of us. It is not cause and effect, but because God is God.

## The Rigour of the Everlasting No

Compare chapter 15:1 – 'The word of the Lord came to Abram *in a vision*.' God's method all through seems to be vision first and then reality. So many mistake the vision for the reality, but in between the vision and the reality there is often a deep valley of humiliation (cf. 15:12 – 'Behold, horror and great darkness fell upon him). How often has a faithful soul been plunged into a like darkness; after the vision has come the test and the darkness. Whenever God gives a vision to a saint, He puts the saint, as it were, in the shadow of His hand, and the saint's duty is to be still and listen. Chapter 16 is an illustration of the danger of listening to good advice when it is dark instead of waiting for God to send the light (cf. Galatians 1:15–16). When God gives a vision and darkness follows, wait; God will bring you into accordance with the vision He has given if you will wait His time. We try to do away with the supernatural in God's undertakings. Never try to help God fulfil His word. There are some things we cannot do, and that is one of them.

Never try to anticipate the actual fulfilment of a vision; you transact some business spiritually with God on your Mount of Transfiguration and by faith see clearly a vision of His purpose, and immediately afterwards there is nothing but blank darkness. You trust in the Lord, but you walk in darkness. The temptation is to work up enthusiasm; you have to stay on God and wait (Is. 50:10–11). If darkness turns to spiritual doldrums, you are to blame. When God puts the dark of 'nothing' into your experience, it is the most positive something He can give you. If you do anything now it is sure to be wrong; you have to remain in the centre of nothing, and say 'thank you' for nothing. It is a very great lesson, which few of us learn, that when God gives us nothing it is because we are inside Him, and by determining to do something we put ourselves outside Him. Abraham would not stay in the land when the famine came because there was nothing; he would not trust God for a child because there was not one. God kept giving Abraham 'nothing', i.e., Himself, and by determining to do something Abraham jumped outside God, and came to find that he was putting himself in the relationship of the everlasting no. There are things God tells us to do without any light or illumination other than just the word of His command, and if we do not obey it is because we are independently strong enough to wriggle out of obeying. All God's commands are enablings, therefore it is a crime to be weak in His strength.

The phrase 'When Abraham was ninety-nine years old' is of immense significance. Thirteen years have rolled by in between chapter 16:16 and chapter 17:1. Abraham had anticipated the purpose of God and had to pass through a long time of discipline. The act of Abraham and Sarah produced a complexity in God's plan all down the ages. So Moses had to wait forty years after his presumptuous attempt to reach his destination. Adam and Eve did the same thing; they took the 'short cut' (which is the meaning of temptation) and anticipated their destination to be *actually* what they were *potentially*—'as God' (Gen. 3:5, RV), and thereby they went wrong. Our destination is to be as God; that is what we are here to become, and in Jesus Christ we do become so. Beware of estimating the temptation of a child of God to be less royal than it really is. The temptation of a child of God does not spring from selfish lust, but from a passionate desire to reach God's destination.

Abraham emerged out of this stage of discipline with one determination, viz., to let God have His way. There is no indication that he is relying on the flesh any longer; his reliance is on God alone. All self-sufficiency has been destroyed in every shape and form; there is not one common-sense ray left as to how God is going to fulfil His word. God never hastens and He never tarries. He works His plans out in His own way, and we either lie like clogs on His hands or we assist Him by being as clay in the hands of the potter.

'*The Lord* appeared to Abram'—the real God now, not a vision. The knowledge of the real God is reached when my confidence is placed in God and not in His blessings. Paul takes Abraham as the type of the life of faith not of sanctification, but of a tried faith built on a real God.

## The Reality of the Everlasting Yes

'I am God Almighty'—El Shaddai, the Father-Mother God, God proved as sufficient for everything. The wonder of El Shaddai (the power to create new things in the old world) runs through the whole kingdom of grace. Remember, Isaac was born of dead parents (Rom. 4:19). If I think I am going to produce the Son of God in myself by prayer, or obedience, or consecration, I am making exaactly the same blunder that Sarah and Abraham made over Hagar. '...who were born...not of the will of the flesh, nor of the will of man, but of God.' Immediately I realize that the thing is impossible, then God will do it. To be brought to the verge of the impossible is to be brought to the margin of the reservations of God. When God is bringing us there we indulge in sulky misbehaviour—'I don't want to go that way; I want your blessings', and when God asks if we have to come to the end of ourselves, we sit resigned and say—'It is all up now', then suddenly we are in paradise because we have come to the end of the thing God could not bring in. The everlasting yes is reached when we perceive that God is El Shaddai, the All-Sufficient God. There is no need so far as God is concerned for the years of silence and discipline if we will only be stupid enough to hear the everlasting no and not try to make it yes—'Oh yes, I am going to try and make my natural virtues pleasing to God'; God says you cannot do it. God does not discard the old and create something entirely new; He creates something in the old until the old and the new are made one. To call conversion new birth is an impoverishment. Because a man who has lived in sin stops sinning, it is no sign that he is born from above. Jesus did not talk about new birth to a sinner, but to a religious man, a godly man full of rectitude; but Nicodemus worshipped God as a reminiscence, he had not the creation of El Shaddai in him. The creation of El Shaddai is what is made possible by the Lord Jesus (Gal. 4:19).

## The Reasonableness of the Everlasting Way

Abraham's faith is to be permanent, that is, he must walk continually before the eyes of the Almighty in the conscious unconsciousness of His presence. We won't walk before God because we are not confident in Him, and the proof that we are not confident in God is that occasionally we get into the sulks. If you are walking with God it is impossible to be in the sulks. Never have the idea that you have disobeyed when you know you have not; the reason you say so is because you are not walking in the permanent light of faith. Suppose Job had said — 'If I were trusting in God I should not be treated like this'; he *was* trusting in God, and he *was* treated like that. Faith is not that I see God, but that I know God sees me; that is good enough for me, I will run out and play — a life of absolute freedom. Watch the spiritual sulks that arise because we want something other than God; we want God to give us something, to make us feel well, to give us wonderful insight into the Bible. That is not the attitude of a saint but of a sinner who is trying to be a saint, and who is coming to God to get things from Him. Unless we give to God the things we get from Him, they will prove our perdition.

## The Rectitude of the Everlasting Day

'And be blameless', free from blame, or guiltless. Abraham was still lacking in the development of his faith and was therefore not blameless as yet. Had Abraham stayed in the land of promise, no matter though he starved to death, he would have been blameless, but he went down to Egypt and so was not blameless. We must beware lest we ignore what the old theologians called prevenient grace, that is, receiving beforehand the grace of God which will keep us worshipping Him instead of trusting in our wits. If we put moral wits in the place of mystic worship, we will go wrong. The life of Abraham does not stand for the life of a saint but for the life of the Father of the Faithful, consequently every error he committed, as well as every glorious thing he did, is recorded and traced out in its consequences through the history of his people. We are not to follow all the steps of Abraham, but to follow the steps of his faith (cf. 1 Corinthians 4:17).

We try to scrape our defects off and say—I think I am all right now. That is not walking blamelessly before God, but walking in determined opposition to faith in God. If I walk in faith in God there will be no specks to rub off; but if I don't walk in faith in God, everything is a defect and a stain, however good I am. It is a snare to continually think about defects, things which we really think should not be there. Imagine anyone who has seen himself in the light of Jesus Christ thinking of his defects! Why we are too filthy for words, and to be concerned because of the spots upon us is absurd. Leave the whole miserable thing alone; we have the sentence of death in ourselves that we should not trust in ourselves but in God, and there are no specks in God. I have determinedly to take no one seriously but God, and the first person I have to leave severely alone as being the greatest fraud I have ever known is myself. 'Oh I am sick of myself' – if you really were sick of yourself you would go to your own funeral and for ever after let God be all in all. Until you get to that point you will never have faith in God.

Beware of the thing that makes you go down before God and sway from side to side spiritually – 'I don't know what to do'; then don't do anything. 'I don't see anything'; well, don't look for anything. 'I thought by this time I should see something'; if you don't, be foolish enough to trust in God. It is the height of madness from common-sense standpoints to have faith in God. Faith is not a bargain with God – I will trust you if you give me money, but not if you don't. We have to trust in God whether He sends us money or not, whether He gives us health or not. We must have faith in God, not in His gifts. Let us walk before God and be blameless, you in your circumstances and I in mine, then we will prove ourselves true children of Abraham.

NINETEEN

# AWE

## *Chapter 17:2–14*

I faced a future all unknown,
No opening could I see,
I heard without the night wind moan,
The days were dark to me—
I cannot face it all alone
O be Thou near to me!

He has, He will, He worketh still,
In ways most wonderful.
He drew me from the miry clay,
He filled my cup quite full.
And while my heart can speak I'll tell
His love unspeakable.

*John Oxenham*

Then Abram fell on his face *(v. 3).*

IT IS SIGNIFICANT to note the times when Abraham did not speak to God but remained silent before Him, not sullen, but silent. Awe is just that—reverential dread and wonder. Beware of its imitation; the pose of reverential awe is the greatest cloak for unbelief. Awe is the condition of a man's spirit realizing who God is and what He has done for him personally. Our Lord emphasizes the attitude of a child; no attitude can express such solemn awe and familiarity as that of a child. In the Apocalypse the attitude of St. John is that of an awestruck child of God.

### THE PERSONAL RELATION IN FAITHFULNESS *(v. 2)*

The covenant with the Father of the Faithful is applicable to every man when once faith (i.e., a relationship between the individual and God) is born. We make covenants with ourselves, or with our experiences, or with our transactions — I came out to the penitent form; or, I surrendered to God. That is a covenant of self-idolatry, an attempt to consecrate our earnest consecration to God. It is never a question of covenanting to keep our vows before God, but of our relationship to God who makes the covenant with us. In the matter of salvation it is God's honour that is at stake, not our honour. Few of us have faith in God; the whole thing is a solemn vow with our religious selves. We promise that we will do what God wants; we vow that we will remain true to Him, and we solemnly mark a text to this effect; but no human being can do it. We have to steadily refuse to promise anything and give ourselves over to God's promise, flinging ourselves entirely on to Him, which is the only possible act of the faith that comes as God's gift. It is a personal relation to God's faith — 'between me and you.' *'Come to me'* said Jesus. The thing that keeps us from coming is religious self-idolatry; we will not let God make a covenant with us, we will make vows with God. Vowing means I can do it if I pledge myself to do it (cf. Exodus 19:8). We have to stake ourselves on the truthfulness of God's character; what He does with us is a matter of indifference. Beware of trusting in your trust and see that you trust in the Lord, and you will never know you trust Him because you are taken up into His certainty.

## The Profound Realization of Fruition *(v. 3)*

'Then Abram fell on his face.' This is an expression of deep humility and trustful confidence and pure joy; these are always the characteristics of faith in God. Every time you say — I feel I haven't got the witness, pack up and get out — out of the compartment of yourself and into the compartment of God, and stay there. Whenever you make a transaction with God, it is real instantly and you have the witness; when there is no witness, no humility, no confidence or joy, it is because you have made a transaction with your religious self and you say — I must wait for God's witness. That is self-idolatry; there is no trust in God in it, but just the mewling of a sick infant. The relation is to be that of a child; fling yourself clean over on to God and wash your hands of the consequences, and John 14:27 — 'My peace I give to you' — becomes true at once. The profound realization of God makes you too unspeakably peaceful to be capable of any self-interest.

## The Precious Recognition of Fellowship *(vv. 3–4)*

'And God talked with him.' The faith that is the creation of God's Spirit in the human soul is never private and personal. When once that faith is created we are caught up into the terrific universal purpose of God, 'You shall be a father of many nations.' The Holy Spirit destroys our personal private life and turns it into a thoroughfare for God. Faith is not the means whereby we take God to ourselves for our select coterie; faith is the gift of God whereby He expresses His purposes through us. God wants to take us up into His purpose so that we no more keep for our joys 'a world within the world', but God can do with us exactly what He likes without saying — By your leave. God does not ask permission to use us any more than we ask permission to use our hands, but we have to keep in joint with God. Full power cannot be put into a machine that is out of gear (cf. 1 John 1:7).

### The Promised Royalty of Fatherhood *(v. 4)*

This amazing promise is exactly expressive of the power of God and it produces moral hysterics. When it begins to dawn in my conscious life what God's purpose is, there is the laughter of the possibility of the impossible. The impossible is exactly what God does. The sure sign that we have no faith in God is that we have no faith in the supernatural. No man can believe God unless God is in him. The promises to Abraham are God all over from beginning to end. Don't only make room for God, but believe that God has room enough for you.

### The Peculiar Recognition of Regeneration Familiarity *(v. 5)*

The new name 'Abraham' announces a new disposition, and circumcision represents the renewal of the whole into a more noble nature by the presence of a new disposition within until the two are made one (cf. Matthew 5:48). Hagar represents not the sinful but the natural, which must first go through the pain of being a willing slave and be turned into oneness with the purpose of God. The difficulty in personal life is that the natural in us says to God in spiteful irritation—I shan't; I won't go back to Sarah; I won't submit to any rule at all, I will boss the whole thing myself. But you cannot; you will either have to come to the death of the natural willingly, or be dragged there by the providential tyranny of God.

## THE PHYSICAL SIGN OF SPIRITUALITY *(vv. 6–14)*

Circumcision, or sanctification which it symbolizes, is the decision to cut away all self-idolatry and abandon to God entirely. The old nature and the new have to be made one, and the sign that they are one is circumcision in the Old Testament and sanctification in the New. The point to remember is that the new creation is made by El Shaddai in the old world. When the Holy Spirit comes in, the two natures are there distinctly, and they have to be amalgamated into one nature. The old has to be turned into a noble nature by the incoming of God; we are not to be fanatical and turn our noses up at the old. The new disposition is the one in which God is all. The Judaisers taught that all those who were of the direct historic seed of Abraham were all right. The Apostle John says no, it is not by physical generation but by supernatural generation (see John 1:12–13). Then came the spiritualizing people who denied that God had anything to do with the physical generation. The Apostle says no. Jesus Christ came that way (see 1 John 4:2), which is a proof that everything that has been defiled is to be made holy through Christ. Beware of insulting God by being a pious prude instead of a pure person.

TWENTY

# ECSTASIED

*Chapter 17:15–27*

Though dim as yet in tint and line,
We trace Thy picture's wise design,
And thank Thee that our age supplies
Its dark relief of sacrifice.
  Thy will be done!
Strike, Thou the Master, we Thy keys,
The anthem of the destinies!
The minor of Thy loftier strain,
Our hearts shall breathe the old refrain,
  Thy will be done!

*Whittier*

Then Abraham fell on his face and laughed *(v. 17)*.

THERE ARE certain phases of the life of faith which look so much like cant and humbug that we are apt to grieve God's Spirit by our religious respectability in regard to them, and ecstasy is just one of those phases. An ecstasied man is one whose state of mind is marked by mental alienation from his surroundings, and his very consciousness is altered into excessive joy. These states are open gateways for God or for the devil. If they are worked up by thrills of our own seeking, they are of the devil; but when they come unsought in faithful performance of duties, they are the gateway into direct communication with God. Ecstasy is not a state in which to live; keep your ecstatic times dark. You have no business to show the depths to anyone but yourself and God.

We are all so abominably serious, so interested in our own characters, that we refuse to behave like Christians in the shallow concerns of life. Our safeguard is the God-given shallowness. It is the attitude of a spiritual prig to go about with a countenance that is a rebuke to others because you have the idea that they are shallower than you. Live the surface common-sense life in a common-sense way, and remember that the shallow concerns of life are as much of God as the profound concerns. It is not our devotion to God or our holiness that makes us refuse to be shallow, but our wish to impress others that we are not shallow, which is a sure sign that we are prigs. We are to be of the stamp of our Lord and Master, and the prigs of His day called Him a glutton and a winebibber; they said He was not dealing with the profound things. Beware of the production of contempt for others by thinking that they are shallow. To be shallow is not a sign of being wicked; the ocean has a shore. The shallow amenities of life are appointed of God and are the things in which our Lord lived, and He lived in them as the Son of God. It is easier for personal pride not to live in them. Beware of posing as a profound person; God became a baby.

## The Princess of God in Human Expression

*(vv. 15, 16)*

The name 'princess' is not earned by piety on the part of the woman; it is the new thing which has been created in her by faith in God. When we find unfortunate ingredients in Abraham and Sarah, and in ourselves, we have to realize that God's designations refer to what He redemptively creates in us, and not to our decorations of ourselves. The treasure is 'in earthen vessels'. A princess in God's sense is not a princess when she prides herself on her own initiative. When our Lord says, 'the same is my sister, and mother', note the condition of His designation, viz., 'he who does the will of My Father in heaven'; not he who has done the will of God once.' Doing the will of God is instantaneously continuous. Am I doing the will of God *now*? Faith does not give us a feeling of eternal life upon which we draw; faith is a fountain of living water overflowing. If I keep living the life of faith then I shall be a sister of the Lord Jesus. There is only one way to live the life of faith, and that is to *live it*.

## The Paradoxes of God and Human Emotion

*(v. 17)*

This is the first time laughter is mentioned in the Bible, and the first mention of a thing in the Bible colours its meaning all the way through. Abraham's laughter had in it no intermixture of wrong. Laughter and weeping are the two intensest forms of human emotion, and these profound wells of human emotion are to be consecrated to God. The devil is never said to laugh. Laughter that is not the laughter of a heart right with God, a child heart, is terrible; the laughter of sin is as the crackling of burning thorns. Whenever the angels come to this earth they come bursting with a joy which instantly has to be stayed (cf. Luke 2:13). This earth is like a sick chamber, and when God sends His angels here He has to say — 'Now be quiet; they are so sick with sin that they cannot understand your hilarity.' Whenever the veil is lifted there is laughter and joy. These are the characteristics that belong to God and God's order of things; sombreness and gloom, oppression and depression, are the characteristics of all that does not belong to God.

The promise was so great that Abraham sank reverently upon the ground, and so paradoxical that he ecstatically laughed – 'Is it to be now at this late day even as you assured me it was to be?' There was no doubt, but amazement; the thing was so completely impossible that Abraham believed it absolutely, so absolutely that his equilibrium was upset. We have all experienced ecstasy in minor degrees. Every time we have transacted business with God on His covenant and have let go entirely on God, there is no sense of merit in it, no human ingredient at all, but such a complete overwhelming sense of being a creation of God's that we are transfigured by peace and joy.

## The Purpose of God and Human Expectation

*(vv. 18–21)*

Abraham was all this time contented with the supposition that Ishmael was the child of promise, but in this new revelation he receives the definite statement of God that Sarah shall bear to him the true heir, and the promise is revealed even in regard to time. Up till now there had been the mingling of doubt with Abraham's faith; he did not trust God completely because he did not see how He was going to fulfil His word. In verse 20 the promise is still more clearly revealed, and with this revelation God withdraws – 'and God went up from Abraham' (v. 22).

## The Programme of God and Human Exercise

*(vv. 22–27)*

These verses state how Abraham complies with the prescribed rite of circumcision. God uses circumcision (as He did the rainbow) and makes it a sign and symbol for something it never was until He made it so. Circumcision becomes with the historic people of God a real sign of the covenant with God that they are His people, but there must be an accompanying sign of our agreement with God. For instance, the physical exertion of coming to a penitent form has a more emphatic meaning than we imagine, and it is against those exertions that human nature protests — 'But it is so humiliating.' Of course it is! If you sit tight against the monitions of the Holy Spirit, you will make yourself obtuse to the voice of God. The thing that keeps you back from obeying is the domination of natural human pride that will not bow to God. Salvation will never be actual until you physically commit yourself to it (Rom. 10:10).

TWENTY-ONE

# FRIEND OF GOD

## *Chapter 18:1–15*

Nor hope to find
A Friend but what has found a Friend in thee! —
All like the purchase; few the price will pay;
And this makes Friends such miracles below.
But since Friends grow not thick on every bough,
Nor ev'ry Friend unrotten at the core;
First on Thy Friend, delib'rate with thyself!
Pause — ponder — sift! not eager in the choice
Nor jealous of the chosen: — fixing, fix!
Judge before Friendship, then confide till death.

*Young*

Do not pass on by your servant *(v. 3).*

THE APOSTLE JAMES calls Abraham 'the Friend of God'. The foundations of friendship with God are laid in inborn qualities; Abraham has that in him now which makes it possible for him to be the friend of God. Never confound 'Saviour' with 'friend'. Our Lord said 'You are my friends' to His disciples, not to sinners. Friendship with God means that there is now something of the nature of God in a man on which God can base His friendship. These inborn qualities are formed in me by the incoming of the Holy Spirit, they are not there by natural generation; then as I obey the revelation granted to me, friendship with God begins, based on the new life which has been created in me. That new life has no affinities on the old lines, but only on the line of God, and is unutterably humble and holy, unsulliedly pure, and absolutely devoted to God. 'El Shaddai'—the One who creates something *in* the old world, and transfigures it.

Friendship with God is faith in action in relation to God and to our fellow men. 'A new commandment I give unto you, that you love one another; even as I have loved you.' I love others as God has loved me, and I see in the ingratitude of others the ingratitude which I have exhibited to God. The fellowship which arises out of such a friendship is a delight to the heart of God.

### The Altar of Fellowship *(vv. 1–5)*

This manifestation of God to Abraham is the most striking sign in the Old Covenant of the Incarnation. The Incarnation in practical identification means the manifestation of God in mortal flesh in every detail of human life. Our Lord was not an ascetic like John the Baptist; He was not limited, or proscribed and fanatical. In our Lord's life the natural and the supernatural were reconciled, the natural was not violently discarded. There was no ostensible preparation for the coming of the Son of God. How many knew that Jesus was God Incarnate? (Jn 1:11–12). It was only when the surgery of events had taken place that their eyes were opened and they knew Him (Lk 24:31). Our Lord comes in the most casual way, and we will miss Him unless we are prepared in our nature to discern Him. The most amazing evidence of a man's nature being changed is the way in which he sees God; to say 'God led me here'; 'God spoke to me'; is an everyday occurrence to him.

The altar of fellowship means that in every occurrence of life I offer myself in devotion to God. Abraham had difficulty at first in bringing the actual details of his life into touch with his real faith in God. Our Lord's actual life was a continual manifestation of His real faith in God; every detail—washing disciples' feet, fasting, praying, marriage feasts—manifested the altar of fellowship.

## The Discipline of Fellowship *(vv. 6–8)*

The reality of God being our Guest is the most awful joy in the discipline of fellowship. The spirit of hospitality consists in this, that in or with the stranger, we receive the Lord Himself. If Abraham could have done more for God actually than he would for any other, his fellowship with God was imperfect; but Abraham did no other for God than he would have done for a stranger, and this is the essential of readiness for God. We do our best to dress ourselves up, we put on behaviour that is not ours, moods that have nothing to do with us, all in order to offer God suitable accommodation. The only way in which we can have God as our Guest is by receiving from Him the Holy Spirit who will turn our bodies into His house. It is not that we prepare a palace for God, but that He comes into our mortal flesh and we do our ordinary work, in an ordinary setting, amongst ordinary people, as for Him. Our Lord teaches that we have to receive those He sends as Himself (Mt. 10:40). When, therefore, we receive hospitality from others in His name, we have to remember that it is being offered to our Master, not to us. It is easier to receive the rebuffs and the spurnings than to receive the hospitality and welcome really offered to our Lord. We say—'But I cannot accept this'; if we are identified with our Lord we will have to go through the humiliation of accepting things of which we feel ourselves unworthy.

Times of feasting reveal a man's master like nothing else in human life, and it is in those times that our Lord reveals Himself to be Master. My treatment of Jesus Christ is shown in the way I eat and drink – I am either a glutton and put Jesus Christ to shame, or else I am an ascetic and refuse to have fellowship with Him in eating and drinking; but when I become a humble saint I reveal Him all the time in the ordinary common ways of life. The ordinance of the Lord's Supper is a symbol of what we should be doing all the time. It is not a memorial of One who has gone, but of One who is always here, 'Do this in remembrance of me' – be in such fellowship with me that you show my death until I manifest myself again. It is in the common things of life that evidence of the discipline of fellowship is given.

## The Illumination of Fellowship *(vv. 9–15)*

'Sarah laughed within herself.' Abraham's laughter was that of joyful faith (17:17); Sarah's laughter was that of doubting little faith. Sarah had to come to the place where her faith was as active as Abraham's, where she was certain that what God had said would happen, would happen. There are times when God seems to overlook certain forms of unbelief; at the other times He brings our unbelief out suddenly into the light and makes us cringe with shame before it. It is not because He wants to show how miserable and mean we are, but because our particular form of unfaith is hindering the expression of His purpose in and through us.

A child of faith must never limit the promise of God by what seems good to him, but must give to the power of God the preference over his own reason. God never contradicts reason, He transcends it always. We 'limit the Holy One of Israel' by remembering what we have allowed Him to do for us in the past; this hinders God and grieves His Spirit. In a time of communion God brings to us a real illumination of His word and we feel thoroughly exhilarated, then we begin to bring in our 'but's'. Whenever you are severely rebuked by God for indulgence in unbelief, take it as an honour from God, because prompt obedience on your part will mean the expression of God's purpose in and through you. The things that burden us either make us laugh at their absurdity, or else make us realize that God is burdening us for His own purpose.

In verses 9 to 14 we have a record of the most remarkable table-talk in the world, the table-talk of God with Abraham and his wife.

TWENTY-TWO

# GETTING THERE

## *Chapter 18:16–33*

If we with earnest effort could succeed
  To make our life one long connected Prayer,
As lives of some perhaps have been and are: —
If — never leaving Thee — we had no need
Our wandering spirits back again to lead
  Into Thy presence, but continued there,
  Like angels standing on the highest stair
Of the sapphire throne — this were to pray indeed!
  But if distractions manifold prevail,
  And if in this we must confess we fail,
Grant us to keep at least a prompt desire,
  Continual readiness for Prayer and Praise —
An altar heaped and waiting to take fire
  With the least spark, and leap into a blaze!

*Trench*

And Abraham came near, and said… *(v. 23).*

'GETTING THERE' means coming into intimate relationship with God without impertinence or lack of reverence. The meaning of intercession is that we see what God is doing; consequently there is an intimacy between the child and the Father which is never impertinent. We must pour into the bosom of God the care which gives us pain and anxiety in order that He may solve for us, and before us, the difficulties which we cannot solve. We injure our spiritual life when we dump the whole thing down before God and say — You do it. That spirit is blind to the real union with God. We must dump ourselves down in the midst of our problems and watch God solve them for us. 'But I have no faith' — bring your problems to God and stay with Him while He solves them, then God Himself and the solution of your problems will be for ever your own. Watch the tendency to pathetic humbug in your approach to God. If we could see the floor of God's immediate presence, we would find it strewn with the 'toys' of God's children who have said — This is broken, I can't play with it any more, please give me another present. Only one in a thousand sits down in the midst of it all and says — I will watch my Father mend this. God must not be treated as a hospital for our broken 'toys', but as our Father.

### The Actual and Real in Union *(vv. 16–19)*

Verse 16 reveals the union of vision and actual life. Abraham sees Jehovah, but he also does his duty to his guests; he does not forget the courtesy of seeing his sublime visitors on their way as if they were ordinary men. The union of the actual and the real was an habitual condition in the life of our Lord; it is not so with us until we learn to make it so. We have a wonderful time of communion with God, then comes the spiritual pout — I have to go and clean boots, or write an essay! In our Lord's life there was no divorce between the actual and the real; He never gave Himself 'continually to prayer'. Beware of the tendency that makes you wish that God would pretend you are someone special; it is a childish make-believe, standing on spiritual tiptoe to look as big as God — others can do this and that, but I must give myself to prayer. The great secret of the obedient life of faith is that the actual conditions of bodily life are transfigured by real communion with God.

'Shall I hide from Abraham what I am doing?' Notice the communing of God with Himself before He gives the revelation to Abraham. God cannot reveal Himself to anyone; the revelations of God are determined by the condition of individual character (cf. Psalm 18:24–26); God takes up the man who is worthy to be the recipient of a revelation. Abraham by his own obedience was fitted to receive the revelation, and this is recognized by God when He brings him into union with Himself, not into absorption, but into complete union.

### The Awful Reckoning Ultimately *(vv. 20–22)*

The moral demand is for the punishment of sin. Every grain of sand cries out for its punishment (cf. Genesis 4:10). Human beings do not echo the cry; only one or two echo it in intercession, and the cry of nature is joined by the man who knows God.

'I will know.' This is the introduction of the final decision. It must become evident in the last trial whether the limit of the long-suffering patience of God has been reached. Verse 22, 'Then the men...', must be connected with chapter 19:1. They were two angels who accompanied Jehovah, and in the form of men they depart to introduce the final test; they depart, but Abraham stands 'yet before the Lord'.

### The Appealing Reverence to the Uttermost *(vv. 23–33)*

There is no impertinence in Abraham's attitude, only profound humility and intensest intimacy. Abraham is not questioning God, but bringing himself to see how God will solve the matter. God allows Abraham to come out with his full intercession until Abraham begins to grasp the essential conditions by which God governs all things. Abraham goes on from step to step, and Jehovah grants him step by step, without once going before his request. The stopping point is reached by reason of the fact that Abraham was in complete communion with God throughout the progress of his intercession. After the final test prayer is impossible (cf. 1 John 5:16).

By means of intercession we understand more and more the way God solves the problems produced in our minds by the conflict of actual facts and our real faith in God. Whenever temptations contend in our minds, and things meet us in the providence of God which seem to involve a contradiction of what we believe, let the conviction of God's righteousness remain unshaken.

It is an insult to sink before God and say 'Your will be done' when there has been no intercession. That is the prayer of impertinent unbelief – there is no use in praying, God does whatever he chooses. The saying of 'Your will be done' is born of the most intimate relationship to God whereby I talk to Him freely. There is in this prayer of Abraham a distinction between the begging which knows no limit and the prayer which is conscious that there are limits set by the holy character of God. Repetition in intercessory importunity is not bargaining, but the joyous insistence of prayer.

The nearer Abraham came to God in his intercession the more he recognized his entire unworthiness – 'Indeed now, I who am but dust and ashes have taken it upon myself to speak to the Lord.' Genuine unworthiness is never shy before God any more than a child is shy before his mother. A child of God is conscious only of his entire dependence upon God.

In the beginning of our spiritual life our prayers are not of faith but of fretfulness. But when you get into the inner place I defy you to go on praying for yourself; it never occurs to you to do so because you are brought into relationship with God who makes your spirit partake of His own. Whenever our Lord spoke of importunity in intercession it was never for ourselves but for others. When by imperceptible degrees we stop praying for ourselves, we are 'getting there'. Prayer is the supreme activity of all that is noblest in our personality, and the essential nature of prayer is faith.

TWENTY-THREE

# SCARCELY SAVED

*Chapter 19:1–29*

Better in bitterest agony to lie,
Before Thy throne,
Than through much increase to be lifted up on high,
And stand alone.

Yet best — the need that broke me at Thy feet,
In voiceless prayer,
And cast my chastened heart, a sacrifice complete,
Upon Thy care.

*John Oxenham*

Escape for your life *(v. 17)*.

It is such chapters as these that enable us to understand the essential nature of God's Redemption.

## Prepared by Gracious Experiences *(vv. 1–3)*

The manifestation which was given to Lot corresponds to that given to Abraham (see 18:2). Lot was not a noble man of God like Abraham, but the fact that he bowed himself to the ground before the angels shows that he retained the power to know when God was near. In comparison with his generation, Lot was righteous, and his contact with Abraham made his manners similar to Abraham's. This preparation by gracious experiences occurs in our personal lives, and such experiences should be cherished for they enable us to do the right thing when we might otherwise do wrong. Beware of not heeding the angel of God in whatever form he comes to you.

'They entered into his house.' The entrance of God into a house does not secure anything, but reveals that there is something there with which God has affinity. It is never our merit God looks at but our faith. If there is only one strand of faith amongst all the corruption within us, God will take hold of that one strand.

After every temptation notice where your affinities lie. If you have gone through the temptation successfully, your affinities will be with the highest and purest (cf. Matthew 4:11); but if you have not the same affinity with the highest, it is a sign that you have become blunted in your spiritual susceptibilities. The seal of doom in a man is that he cannot believe in purity, and this can only be accounted for by an internal twist; no man gets there easily. What is true in individual lives has become appallingly true in Sodom.

God has given us a precious gift in that looking at other Christians we see not them but the Lord. If you see only where others are *not* the Lord, it is you who are wrong, not they; you have lost the bloom of spirit which keeps you in touch with Jesus Christ. If I cannot see God in others, it is because He is not in me. If I get on my moral high horse and say it is they who are wrong, I become that last of all spiritual iniquities, a suspicious person, a spiritual devil dressed up as a Christian. Beware of mistaking suspicion for discernment; it is the biggest misunderstanding that ever twisted Christian humility into Pharisaism. When I see in others things that are not of God, it is because the Spirit of God has revealed to me my own meanness and badness; when I am put right with God on the basis of His Redemption and see those things in others, it is in order that God may restore them through my intercession. Be careful never to lose the bloom of your spiritual susceptibilities.

## Proposals of Great Evil *(v. 4)*

The history of Sodom reveals that sin is the beginning of the most appalling corruption. Always distinguish between what we are apt to call sin and what the Bible calls sin. The Bible does not call the corruption of Sodom sin; sin is a disposition, not a deed. The corruption of Sodom is the criminal result of sin. It is because this distinction has been lost sight of that pseudo-evangelical preaching has been to the effect that only moral blackguards can be saved. When our Lord faced men not guilty of moral blackguardism, but worthy, upright men, He did not deal with them in the way He did with sinners; He seemed to be infinitely sterner with the Pharisees than with the publicans (see Matthew 21:31). He looked at something we do not see, viz., the disposition.

Lot was the only one who stood as a representative of God in Sodom, and while he was free from the abominations of Sodom, he was not far from its worldly mind. His was the doubting heart which soon turns to double ways. Lot's position arises from having borrowed most of his piety (Gen. 12:4). Weak faith chooses the visible things instead of enduring as seeing Him who is invisible, and slowly and surely such faith settles down between mammon and righteousness. In the supreme test Lot trusted his wits; Abraham worshipped and waited.

## Perils of Grievous Emotion *(vv. 5–9)*

In the history of Sodom independence of God reaches the limit of blasphemy. The way to get there in personal life is to indulge in sentimental spirituality. If you indulge in a spiritual sentiment you do not intend to obey, the exact opposite of that emotion will come in its wake. Beware of panic, because panic always advocates doing wrong that right may result. In fact, the tendency to *do* instead of to devote one's self to God, is nearly always the sin of a smudged purity of relationship to God.

## Performance of God's Ends *(vv. 10–29)*

Abraham standing alone with God is the key to the rescue of Lot and his family; out they come whether they like it or not. The angels are insistent in answer to Abraham's intercession (see verse 16). Yet Lot was rescued with the greatest difficulty because of his vacillation. Vacillation in a crisis is the sign of an unabandoned nature. An abandoned nature never can vacillate because there is nothing to weigh; such a nature is completely abandoned to another. Lot's fear was culpable because it was indicative of a stultified judgement.

See to it that you do not profane the holiness of God by refusing to abandon yourself away from your experience of what He has done for you to God Himself. Whenever you do not come in contact with God for yourself, you will begin to watch your own whiteness—I dare not say this or do that. It is a cabined, confined life and when difficulties come like a wall of fire, God has to come and rescue you; and He does it by means of intercession on the part of someone else. Beware of accepting the blessings and visions of God as an indication of your goodness and not of the mercy and purpose of God – 'the Lord being merciful to him' (v. 16).

TWENTY-FOUR

# WRECKED IN HARBOUR

*Chapter 19:30–38*

A Chequer-Board of mingled Light and Shade?
And We the Pieces on it deftly laid?
Moved and removed, without a word to say,
By the Same Hand that Board and Pieces made?

No Pieces we in any Fateful Game,
Nor free to shift on Destiny the blame;
Each Soul doth tend its own immortal flame,
Fans it to Heaven, or smothers it in shame.

*John Oxenham*

And he dwelt in a cave *(v. 30)*.

THE PHRASE 'wrecked in harbour' describes the character that has gone through great storms and has made the harbour, and yet is wrecked as the result of an inward, persisting defect.

> I am very sorry for the failures at Christchurch of which you tell. I suspect that cleverness was at the bottom of the failure, for it is a character of mind the exercise of which is so instantly and pleasantly rewarded, that the temptation to cultivate it is always present.
>
> *Sir James Paget in a letter to his son*

Spiritual cleverness is the cause of much of our failure. We may not have much mental cleverness, but some of us are dexterously clever spiritually. We have so many memories of the times when God came in and did the thing that we determinedly 'loaf' on God – only we call it 'relying on the Holy Spirit'. There are times when God does give real spiritual insight and times when He does not, and if between the times of inspiration you do not work but 'loaf', you are leading up to tremendous failure one day. The moments of light and inspiration are an indication of the standard which we must work to keep up. If between the times of inspiration we refuse to practise, we shall fail spiritually exactly where Paget's son failed intellectually. He failed because he trusted to the clever moments of his genius, and we fail because we trust to the moments of spiritual cleverness.

## The Natural History of the Prudence Peril

The prudence which appears in the life of Abraham as sinful prudence (e.g., 12:10) appears again in the lives of his kindred, and is the persisting defect in the character of Lot. No man can do things and leave them with himself. He may not see the result, but he will have to answer for it generations after. The prudence peril is traceable first of all in Adam, then in Noah, then in Abraham, and right on to the end of the chapter until it becomes the most dominant characteristic of Israel and Judah. The terror of the prudence peril is that it can end in such a deed as this. These things are written for our instruction. 'But I never could do such things.' What any man has ever done, any man can do if he does not watch.

The error is putting prudence in competition with God's will, weighing *pros* and *cons* before God when He has spoken. Always beware when you want other people to commend the decision you have made, because it is an indication that you have trusted your wits instead of worshipping God. If you say 'But I can prove I was right', you may be sure you are wrong, because you have to use your ingenuity to prove you are right. When you act in faith in God it is not logical proof that you are right that matters, but the certainty of the divine approval, and this keeps you from seeking the approval of others. We have to watch that we use our wits to assist us in worshipping God and carrying out His will, not in carrying out our own will and then asking God very piously to bless the concoction. Put communication with God on the throne, and then ask God to direct your common sense to choose according to His will. Worship first and wits after.

## The Natural History of Panic Perversity

Sensual passion always follows spent panic. It is easy to fall into the sins of the flesh when once the ideals of life lose their power. All you have to do is to get into a panic on any line, and you will be as perverse as can be because you have committed a sin against your own nature. Not only so, but you have given an opportunity to the devil over your body. There was an entire absence of panic in the life of our Lord, consequently nothing of the nature of perversity. Notice how our Lord continually curbed Peter on the line of impulse, because impulse is apt to lead to panic, and anything of the nature of panic opens the door to perversity and sensuality. A saint has no right to give way to a panic of nerves; it is a deliberate giving way and has to be halted up instantly. When we give way to a panic of nerves we give the temple of the Holy Spirit over to the devil. Beware of the 'panickiness' which takes the form of hysteria, because on the borders of hysteria lurk all the demons that can possess human nature.

Never sympathize with anyone who is giving way to hysteria; if you do, you aid and abet Satan in thrusting the temple of the Holy Spirit into the clutches of the devil.

Never allow an emotion which you know you dare not carry out on its own level; grip it on the threshold of your mind in a vice of blood and allow it no more way. Few of us realize the power we have of doing this. I am a criminal in the sight of God for allowing an emotion with regard to anyone which I know I dare not carry out on its logical level. If once we got hold of the psychological law that an emotion not carried out on its legitimate level will react on a lower level, it would bring the wind of rugged reality into devotional meetings. It is possible to step from devotion to God into a moral cesspool in one second, and we are to blame before God for not knowing these things. God's word is as rugged and unvarnished as can be on this line, and it is the cunning and abominable nonsense of what is called good taste that prevents these things being stated. I have no business to allow false emotions before God, emotions that are not 'me' at all, and that I have not the remotest intention of carrying out. Our Lord requires not only chastity of body, He requires chastity of thought.

> The law that every extraordinary expansion or satisfaction of heart or brain or will is paid for, paid for inevitably without the possibility of putting off or transferring the payment, is one of the truths about which no human being with a soul a little above the brute has the slightest doubt.... It is an eternal and immutable verity and the soul of man is a witness to it.
>
> *'The Law of Nemesis' (Prof. Saintsbury)*

TWENTY-FIVE

# PHILISTINISM

*Chapter 20:1–7*

When the powers of hell prevail
  O'er our weakness and unfitness,
Could we lift the fleshly veil,
  Could we for a moment witness
    Those unnumbered hosts that stand
    Calm and bright on either hand –
Oh! what joyful hope would cheer!
  Oh! what faith serene would guide us!
Great may be the danger near,
  Greater are the friends beside us.

And Abraham journeyed...and sojourned in Gerar *(v. 1).*

THE TERM 'Philistinism' owes its popularity to Matthew Arnold and is used today in reference to uncultured people. It is used here because this is the first meeting of the house of Abraham with the Philistines, and also because at this stage Abraham lapsed into uncultured confidence in himself and into compromise with spiritually uncultured people. To say 'I can't understand how Abraham could do it' is self-deception. If you will look inside your own heart, provided you do not love yourself too much, you will never say such a thing. We have to be careful lest we blind ourselves by putting up our own standards instead of looking at the standard God puts up. If we put a saint up as a standard, we blind ourselves to ourselves; it is personal vanity makes us do it. When we put God's standard up, viz., Himself, there is no room for personal vanity. It is self-deception to say – 'Because I am saved and sanctified, therefore all I do is sure to be right.' As long as I establish myself amongst people who agree with me and am consciously 'bigger' than them all, it is easy to be complacent; but when circumstances oust me out amongst another set of people who do not accept my standards, my complacency is upset and I am nowhere. The grace of God makes us honest with ourselves. We must be humorous enough to see the shallow tricks we all have, no matter what our profession of Christianity. We are so altogether perverse that God Almighty had to come and save us! Whenever we forget this and begin to set up little standards of our own, imbedded in some favourite saint, we are sure to go wrong. We have to get rid of all notions about ourselves and our own standards, and keep in front what God puts in front, viz., our Lord Himself, then we will not be tempted to delusion about ourselves. Our eye must be on God, not on ourselves.

## THE DISPOSITION OF REACTION *(v. 1)*

When the Bible records facts of experience, look in your own experience for the answer; when the Bible reveals standards of revelation, look to God, not to experience.

The reaction from a state of great spiritual excitement is revealed in Abraham as well as in Lot, and as on a former occasion (see 12:10) Abraham decides to change his residence – 'and he sojourned in Gerar'. If we bring the light of experience to this reaction on the part of Abraham, we shall understand how even such a believer as he fell the second time into the same sin. We are apt to say—'I won't do that thing again now that God has warned me.' But you will; you will do it as certainly as Abraham did if you trust to your vows instead of to God. The one thing to do is to look steadfastly to God. Always beware when you are perfectly certain you are right, so certain that you do not dream of asking God's counsel. God never puts the judgement with our wits, but entirely with Himself, consequently we must never depend on our moral judgement or our intellectual discernment, or on our sense of right and justice. All these are right in themselves but not right in us; we can only be right as we remain absolutely confident in God. When we realize that we have repeated a sin, the danger is to lie down in the mud and refuse to get up. There is no refuge in vowing or in praying, but only in one place, in absolute confidence in God. The child attitude is the only right one.

### The Discretion of Reason *(v. 2)*

Judged from every standpoint, it would seem the right thing for Abraham to get away from the blasted country of Sodom and go to Gerar. It was not wrong from any standpoint—it was the act of a wise, sensible, reasoning man of God; but Abraham was not God's man in going because immediately he goes God rebukes him. In going to Gerar, as in going down to Egypt, Abraham thought he was justified, but in each case an entirely different thing happens from what he intended, viz., Sarah is taken from him. Whenever we bring in our ordinary wisdom as a factor of decision on any point, we are 'out of it', not morally or with human beings (it will end with a wrong relation to human beings ultimately), but our relationship to God is injured. Abraham had no notion that he was doing wrong to Abimelech, but the record proves that he did, and also that he injured his relationship to God as a faithful soul. Beware of being other than a simple child of God. The only safeguard is dependence upon God, not on godly decisions.

Beware whenever your logical moral right puts you in a wrong relation to God. 'If God will only prove that my right is right' — it is the one thing over which we are stubbornly jealous of God. 'I know I am right,' we say, and it has to be proved to us that from the standpoint of the Holy Spirit we are wrong. If I can prove to my own mind that I am right, by that very act I am wrong in disposition towards God.

## THE DREAM OF REALIZATION *(v. 3)*

The fact that God makes good come out of my wrong does not make my wrong any better; I have simply utilized God's permissive will to go in a circle when I should have gone straight. There are times when you see what God wants and you begin to obey with the simple direct obedience of a child; then comes the 'choppy waters' of friends' advice or of considerations of yourself, and for a while you wobble because you have become discreet and shrewd and wise, instead of being a child of God. Then when after the passing of days, or longer, according to your stubbornness, God brings you out of all the turmoil, the devil comes and says it was a good thing after all. It was not, it was a bad thing. You prevented God's order being worked out directly through you, and He had to allow you to go in a circle and only brought you back after having grieved you through with sorrows.

Beware of justifying yourself when God alone is the justifier. If ever I can justify myself, I make God unjust. If I am right and morally based in all I do and say, I do not need a Saviour, and God is not justified in the extravagant waste of sending Jesus Christ to die for me. If God judges me a sinner who needs saving, and I can prove that I am just, I make God unjust (cf. Psalm 51:4). Every kind of upholding I give to myself, whether I be saint or sinner, is a blow in the face of God, and is a proof that I am on the wrong basis. If in any detail I take the justice of God and make it mean my own justice, I thereby prove God to be unjust. This is part of the mystery of godliness and can only be understood by the intuition of faith (Mt. 11:25).

### The Dilemma of Rectitude *(vv. 4–7)*

God stepped in and delivered Abimelech from committing sin because of His sheer mercy – 'I also withheld you from sinning against me.' There is a difference between deliverance from sin by God's sovereign act, which is an occasion for praise, and the defiance of sin by personal integrity, which tells in the building up of character. There are times in personal life when God by His sovereign act prevented us from committing sin, and when we look back and see how He preserved us, the danger is to say it must have been because of our innocence. No, it was of the mercy of God.

We have to learn to utilize a right reliance on circumstances in the spiritual domain, to discern that it is God who engineers circumstances. Abraham refused to see this, and every now and again he stepped in and engineered circumstances for himself, and every time he did this, he upset everything. Reverent humility and moral pride are ultimately brought out very clearly – the former in Abraham and the latter in Abimelech. The believer in his weakness is exalted above the man of the world in his strength.

TWENTY-SIX

# HUMILIATION

*Chapter 20:8–18*

Sink in thou blessèd sign!
  Pass all my spirit through
And sever with thy sacred touch
  The hollow from the true.

Through my heart's very ground
  Thy ploughshare must be driven,
Till all are better loved than self,
  And yet less loved than heaven.

And Abraham said, Because... *(v. 11).*

HUMILIATION AND humility must not be confounded. Humility can never be humiliated. To be humiliated means to be lowered on condition. The word as applied to our Lord has no reference whatever to His personal calibre, but to the lowering of His external form from *'being in the form of God'* to *'taking the form of a servant'*. Humiliation as applied to us means a lowering of condition in the sense of being mortified. Whenever we pride ourselves on anything as being of real acceptance to God and realize that He absolutely ignores that thing, we will experience the ghastly humbling of humiliation.

## THE HUMILITY AND HONOUR OF ABIMELECH
*(vv. 8–10)*

Abimelech's true humility is revealed in the way he humbles himself in communicating the events of his dream to his courtiers; he deliberately makes known before his whole court the compromising position he is in. Verse 8 describes the intense publicity of his confession, and verses 9 to 11 his rigorous, yet not vindictive talk with Abraham—although there is stinging irony in what he says to Sarah (v. 16).

In nine cases out of ten, reserve is simply personal pride, which will turn to insolence or iniquity at a moment's notice. One of the most delicate issues in the history of the human soul is that of concealing what ought to be made known and of making known what ought to be concealed. When concealing is a great relief, question it; when revealing is a great relief, question it. The only guiding factor is obedience to the highest we know. The wriggling we indulge in to escape from being humiliated prevents our being right with God. For instance, you have a wrong attitude of mind towards another, and the Spirit of God tells you to put it right between yourself and that one (cf. Matthew 5:24), and you say—No, I will put it right between myself and God. You cannot do it; it is impossible. Instead of deliberately obeying God, irrespective of what it costs, we use the trick of prayer to cover our own cowardice. It is a very subtle subterfuge to prevent ourselves being humiliated, but God will bring us into a place of humiliation externally, and others will see we are humiliated. If, on the other hand, there is something between yourself and God, and you feel it would be an enormous relief to tell someone else about it, *don't.* 'I did not immediately confer with flesh and blood.' It is never a question of giving an explanation to someone else, but of maintaining obedience to the highest we know at all costs.

Personal misconduct will never bring bondage on others unless the misconduct springs from an independent attitude of mind towards God. Wrongdoing on the part of any student here will never interfere with the atmosphere unless along with the misconduct there is a deliberate defiance of mind against God, then the whole atmosphere of the college will be charged with antagonism, and the antagonism will last as long as that one remains at 'loggerheads' with God spiritually. It is not wrongdoing but a wrong attitude of mind towards God spiritually that damages the atmosphere.

It was independence of God on the part of Abraham that brought the trouble on the house of Abimelech. Abraham repeated the mistake of a former occasion because of a wrong attitude to God; he was so wrong that he thought he was doing right. Abimelech had reason to complain of the conduct of Abraham in the same way that Pharaoh had reason to complain of it (cf. 12:13–20), and Abimelech does not shrink from declaring his injured sense of truth and justice. Imagine the humiliation it would be to Abraham when he realized what he had done.

## The Humiliation and Honour of Abraham

*(vv. 11–18)*

The way in which Abraham offers his apologies reveals clearly that he was ashamed. The fear of man which had determined him earlier (12:11–13) was awakened afresh in him by what he had so recently seen in Sodom, and he was suspicious of human nature everywhere—'Because I thought surely the fear of God is not in this place.' Abraham ashamedly explains his motive and gives his explanation for his equivocation. In verse 12 he explains that what he said of Sarah was not untrue, but he also indicates that his reason for saying she was his sister has deservedly brought him into humiliation. There was none of the sneakish element in Abraham as there was in Jacob; his reason for denying his wife was that through her God had promised him a child, and he was trying to guard her for God.

We are always in danger of mistaking personal predilections for Christian perfection, and we have to learn to take the veil off our moral quirks. Over and over again it works like this: we begin to be cunning and think—Now, if I am not careful that man will utilize my position for his own purposes. The real reason we say it is that we do not like that particular man and imagine therefore that God does not like him either. Or else it works in this way: when someone whom we like comes, we say—Oh yes, that is of God's order; but I can't be bothered with those other people, I do not think God guided them to come. It is the same old trick, and we have to be excessively careful that we do not lean to our own understanding and try to conserve God's order in our way instead of allowing God to conserve His order in His own way.

There was never any element of fear or cunning or diplomacy in our Lord in any shape or form. Our Lord was never suspicious of anyone; yet He trusted no one saving His Father, consequently He was never vindictive, nor was He ever humiliated. It is only possible to be humiliated when we are serving our own pride.

Abraham's defects are clear and his sins obvious, but his nobility is extraordinary. Abraham is never presented as a saint or as a type of sanctification. Phases of his life may be used to present these, but Abraham himself is the type of the life of faith in its failures and in its successes. Sanctification is not something our Lord does in me; sanctification is *Himself* in me. 'But of him you are in Christ Jesus, who became for us...sanctification' (1 Cor. 1:30).

TWENTY-SEVEN

# GOD IS GOOD

## *Chapter 21:1–8*

Never to be again! But many more of the kind
As good, nay, better perchance: is this your comfort to me?
To me, who must be saved because I cling with my mind
To the same, same self, same love, same God: ay, what was, shall be.

There shall never be one lost good! What was, shall live as before;
The evil is null, is nought, is silence implying sound;
What was good shall be good, with, for evil, so much good more;
On the earth the broken arcs; in the heaven, a perfect round.

*Browning*

God has made me to laugh *(v. 6)*.

ONE OF THE greatest demands of God on the human spirit is to believe that God is good when His providence seems to prohibit the fulfilment of what He has promised. The one character in the Bible who sustains this strain grandly is Abraham. Paul, in summing up the life of Abraham, points to it as his greatest quality—'Abraham believed God.'

## God's Performance of His Own Promise *(v. 1)*

No one can fulfil a promise but the one who made it. These words contain the whole autobiography of the godly ups and downs of the life of faith. During the years when everything seemed to contradict the fulfilment of the promise, Abraham continually forgot this fundamental fact and tried to help God fulfil it. God alone can fulfil His promise, and we have to come to the place of perfect reliance upon God (cf. 1 Thessalonians 5:23–24).

'The Lord visited Sarah as he had said, and the Lord did for Sarah as he had spoken' (v. 1). God visits the believer with the word of promise and visits him again with the word of fulfilment. Abraham endured for twenty-five years without any sign of fulfilment. The majority of us know nothing about waiting; we don't wait, we endure. Waiting means that we go on in the perfect certainty of God's goodness — no dumps or fear. The attitude of the human heart towards God who promises should be to give Him credit for being as honest as He ought to be, and then to go on in the actual life as if no promise had been made. That is faithful waiting.

## God's Presentation of His Own Performance *(v. 2)*

The presentation of God's performance here is in the actual details of the birth of an ordinary child, extraordinary only to the eye of faith. We come to God not with faith in His goodness but with a conception of our own, and we look for God to come to us in that way. God cannot come to me in my way, He can only come in His own way — in ways man would never dream of looking for Him. In the Incarnation the Eternal God was so majestically small that He was not detected; the world never saw Him. And this is true in regard to us; God is so insignificant providentially, that we never see Him. We cry out – 'Oh God, I wish you would come to me' when He is there all the time, and suddenly we see Him and say 'Surely the Lord is in this place; and I did not know it.' We looked for desolation and anguish, and instead there is the laughter and hilarity of realizing that we see God. This astonishment at the performance of God is brought out over and over again until we learn to be humiliated at our despicable disbelief. 'I don't know what I am going to do in the coming months' – but I thought you knew God! Have all these days and weeks gone by and has God shown you nothing? Your anxiety proves that you do not believe in the goodness of God an atom, and it postpones the time of His performance.

## God's Programme for His Progeny *(vv. 3–8)*

What Abraham did for his son was in accordance with God's programme for him, not according to Abraham's ways for him (cf. Proverbs 22:6). God has a distinct programme for every child born into this world, legitimately or illegitimately. If the programme is unheeded, the reason is that parents do not care about God's programme being fulfilled, but it will be fulfilled all the same. In spiritual matters be careful to note God's programme for His progeny in you. Is the Son of God formed in me? Have I heard God's promise about Him? He 'shall be called the Son of God' (Lk. 1:35), that is, He has nothing to do with my natural abilities. There is no relation between the promise of God for the life He forms in us by regeneration and our personal private ambitions; those ambitions are completely transfigured. I have to heed the promise of God for my child, be it a child of nature or of grace, and see that I do not try to make God's gift fulfil my own ends. If I do, I become cruel in my judgement of God and God has to be very severe with me.

Suppose that God sees fit to put you into desolation when He begins the forming of His Son in you; what does it matter to you, and what ought it to matter? God's programme was to look after Sarah only until the child of His promise was born, and all He is after in you and me is the forming of His Son in us. When He drives the sword through the natural, we begin to whine and say 'Oh, I can't go through that', but we must go through it. If we refuse to make our natural life obedient to the Son of God in us, the Son of God will be put to death in us. We have to put on the new man in our human nature to fit the life of the Son of God in us, and see that in the outer courts of our bodily lives we conduct our life for Him.

'God has made me laugh.' Sarah's hilarity is the joy of God sounding through the upset equilibrium of a mind that scarcely expected the promise to be fulfilled. The son of Sarah is himself a type of the Son of Mary, and in each case the promise is limited through a particular woman, and through an apparently impossible, yet actual birth. Fancy making everything depend on that haughty, inclined-to-be-unstable, not amazingly-superb-in-rectitude Sarah! How haphazard God seems, not sometimes but always. God's ways turn man's thinking upside down.

Verse 7 is indicative of the amazement that comes when God's promise is fulfilled. What is known as the dark side of Christian experience is not really Christian experience at all; it is God putting the rot of sacramental death through the natural virtues in order to produce something in keeping with His Son, and all our whining and misery ought to be the laughter of Sarah — Now I see what God wants! Instead of that, we moon in corners and gloom before God, and say 'I am afraid I am not sanctified.' If you fight against the desolation, you will kill the life of God in you; yield to it, and God's fulfilment will amaze you. It is in the periods of desolation that the sickly pietists talk about 'What I am suffering!' They are in the initial stages and have not begun to realize God's purpose. God is working out the manifestation of the fulfilment of His promise, and when it is fulfilled there is never any thought of self or of self-consideration anywhere.

TWENTY-EIGHT

# WHICH?

*Chapter 21:9–21*

Profit? – Loss?
Who shall declare this good – that ill?
When good and ill so intertwine
But to fulfil the vast design
Of an Omniscient Will? –
When seeming gain but turns to loss, –
When earthly treasure proves but dross, –
And what seemed loss but turns again
To high, eternal gain?

*John Oxenham*

But God said, Do not let it be displeasing in your sight *(v. 12).*

THE DILEMMAS of our personal life with God are few if we obey and many if we are wilful. Spiritually the dilemma arises from the disinclination for discipline; every time I refuse to discipline my natural self, I become less and less of a person and more and more of an independent, impertinent individual. Individuality is the characteristic of the natural man; personality is the characteristic of the spiritual man. That is why our Lord can never be defined in terms of individuality, but only in terms of personality. Individuality is the characteristic of the child, it is the husk of the personal life. It is all 'elbows' – it separates and isolates; personality can merge and be blended. The shell of individuality is God's created covering for the protection of the personal life, but individuality must go in order that the personal life may be brought out into fellowship with God – 'that they may be one, even as we are one.'

## THE OFFENCE OF THE NATURAL *(vv. 9–10)*

Sarah is full of indignation when she sees the mocking of Ishmael, and begs Abraham to 'cast out this bondwoman and her son'. God tells Abraham to hearken to what Sarah says, and Ishmael is cast out. We have to remember, however, that Sarah gave Hagar to Abraham to be his wife; we always become anxious when we take our own self-chosen ways. In the Epistle to the Galatians the Apostle Paul makes his great revelation regarding that which was 'born after the flesh' and that which was 'born after the Spirit'. He is dealing not with sin, but with the relationship between the natural and the spiritual. The natural must be disciplined and turned into the spiritual by sacrifice (cf. Galatians 5:24), otherwise it will produce a tremendous divorce in the life. Why did God make it necessary for the natural to be sacrificed to the spiritual? God did not. God's order was that the natural should be transformed into the spiritual by obedience; sin made it necessary for the natural to be sacrificed to the spiritual, and that after sanctification, remember. We have the idea that sanctification means deliverance from sin only; it means much more. It means that we start on a life of discipline such as nine out of every ten of us will have nothing to do with.

The offence of the natural is its robust ridicule of the spiritual, and if the natural is not 'cast out' it will not only perish itself but will lead the whole personal life astray. 'I was not disciplined when I was a child.'

You must discipline yourself now; if you do not, you will ruin your life for God. If the natural is not sacrificed to the spiritual by me, not by God, it will mock at the life of the Son of God in me and produce a continual 'swither' (indecisive agitation), which is always the result of an undisciplined nature. Instead of 'I can't', say *'I won't'*, and you have it exactly; it is the Ishmael jeer. People go wrong spiritually because they stubbornly refuse to discipline themselves physically, mentally or in any way, and after a while they become that most contemptible and objectionable thing, a petted man or woman, and their own greatest cause of suffering. There is no suffering to equal the suffering of self-love arising from independent individuality which refuses to submit either to God or to its nobler self.

### THE OFFERING OF THE NATURAL *(vv. 11–13)*

The casting out of the bondwoman and her son was necessary not only for the line of promise but for the welfare of Ishmael himself. All the problems regarding civilization and organization and the natural virtues arise along this line. If I put the civilized organization to which I belong, or my natural virtues, on the throne, they will make a mock of the Son of God who is formed in me. These things are the outcome of the natural life and I have to resolutely put them under, not because they are wrong, but because they are individual protests against the life of the Son of God in me. The natural life is not spiritual; it can only be made spiritual by deliberately casting it out and making it the slave instead of the ruler. My business is to make independent individuality conform to the Son of God in me by severity. We are apt to deify wilfulness and independence and call them by the wrong name; what we call strength of will God looks upon as contemptible weakness. The Being with the greatest will who ever lived on the earth was our Lord Jesus Christ, and yet He never exercised His will, as we think of will; His life was one of meekness and submission (see John 5:19, 30). Our Lord was the antipodes of the individual; there was nothing independent or wilful or self-assertive about Him, and He says 'Learn from me, for I am gentle and lowly in heart.' Jesus Christ cannot give me a meek and quiet spirit — I have to take His yoke upon me; that is, I have to deliberately discipline myself. The teaching of the Sermon on the Mount is the destruction of individuality and the exaltation of personality. When the personal life is merged with God, it will manifest the characteristics of God. Individuality never exhibits the characteristics of God but natural characteristics, the characteristics of Ishmael, or of Esau, or of Saul of Tarsus, that mock at the meek and lowly Son of God. What is it that begins to mock in you? 'Meek? Do you think I am going to bow my neck to that? Be loyal there, in my home? Obey a passing sentiment that came to me in a prayer meeting?' Cast out 'the bondwoman and her son' — the natural life and all that nourishes it, or it will lead your personal life to ruin. The casting out must be done by you, then God will bring it back into its rightful inheritance. The natural life can only be brought into union by being cast out (cf. Matthew 5:29, 48).

If we do not resolutely cast out the natural, the supernatural can never become natural in us. There are some Christians in whom the supernatural and the natural seem one and the same, and you say — Well, they are not one with me, I find the natural at 'loggerheads' with the spiritual. The reason is that the other life has gone through the fanatical stage of cutting off the right arm, gone through the discipline of maiming the natural, completely casting it out, and God has brought it back into its right relationship with the spiritual on top, and the spiritual manifests itself in a life which knows no division into sacred and secular. There is no royal road there – each one has it entirely in his own hands; it is not a question of praying but of performing.

### The Ostracism of the Natural *(v. 14)*

The casting out of Hagar and Ishmael is necessary, but Hagar is not divorced. Divorce stands for apostasy (cf. Isaiah 50:1). We must be *divorced* from sin, not separated from sin. Sin belongs to hell and the devil; I, as a child of God, belong to heaven and God, and I must have nothing to do with sin in any shape or form. The separation which goes on all through the life of faith is alluded to by Paul in Galatians 2:20 – 'I have been crucified with Christ'; and again in Romans 12:1 – 'Present your bodies a living sacrifice' – go to the funeral of your own independence. It is not a question of giving up sin, but of giving up my right to myself, my natural independence and self-assertiveness. Immediately I do, the natural cries out and goes through terrific suffering. There are things in me which must go through death or they will remain alone and ruin the personal life (cf. John 12:24). But if I sternly put them through death, God will bring them back into the right inheritance. Jesus says 'If any man will be my disciple, let him deny himself', i.e., deny his right to himself, and a man has to realize who Jesus Christ is before he will do it. It is the things that are right and noble and good from the natural standpoint that keep us back from God's best. To discern that the natural virtues antagonize surrender to God is to begin to see where the battle lies. It is going to cost the natural everything, not something.

## The Ordeal of the Natural *(vv. 15–18)*

Beware of blaspheming the Creator by calling the natural sinful. The natural is not sinful, but un-moral and unspiritual. It is the home of all the vagrant vices and virtues, and must be disciplined with the utmost severity until it learns its true position in the providence of God. Remember, Abraham had to offer up Ishmael before he offered up Isaac. Some of us are trying to offer spiritual sacrifices before we have sacrificed the natural. The only way we can offer a spiritual sacrifice to God is to do what He tells us to do, discipline what He tells us to discipline. Under no consideration must we dictate to God on the basis of the natural life. When God's Son tells me to do a thing, I have no business to allow the natural to dictate and say — I cannot do that because I get so tired. What does it matter if it kills the natural? God's purpose for the natural will be fulfilled; I have to be absolutely stern with it and not make God wait on my natural inclinations.

## The Outrance of the Natural *(vv. 19–21)*

'Outrance' — the utmost extremity or bitter end. Verse 20 is striking — 'God was with the lad', as long as he remained in the straits of the desert, and he found his home in the oases and by the wells. After Ishmael had learned by experience that he was not a fellow heir with Isaac, he was richly endowed by Abraham, and he also remained in friendly relationship with Isaac (25:9). God is not with my natural life as long as I pamper it and pander to it, but when I put it out in the desert, resolutely cast it out and keep it under, then God is with it and He opens up wells and oases, and fulfils His promise for it. It must be stern discipline, rigorous severity to the last degree on my part (cf. 1 Corinthians 9:27), then God will be with the natural life and bring it to its full purpose.

TWENTY-NINE

# CONDITIONS

## *Chapter 21:22–34*

Now, who shall arbitrate?
Ten men love what I hate,
Shun what I follow, slight what I receive;
Ten, who in ears and eyes
Match me: we all surmise,
They this thing, and I that: whom shall my soul believe?

But I need, now as then,
Thee, God, who mouldest men;
And since, not even while the whirl was worst,
Did I, — to the wheel of life
With shapes and colours rife,
Bound dizzily, — mistake my end, to slake Thy thirst.

*Borwning*

Thus they made a covenant at Beer-sheba *(v. 32).*

THE LIFE of faith as portrayed in the life of Abraham is a detailed presentation of its majesties and its muddles. We have detected Abraham's blunder in the actual conditions in working from his wits, but we must not forget that by far the most striking thing about Abraham is his worship of God.

In this chapter the right relation between common sense and faith is exhibited. Common sense is not faith and faith is not common sense; they stand in the relation of Ishmael and Isaac, of the natural and the spiritual, of individuality and personality, of impulse and inspiration. Faith in antagonism to common sense is fanaticism, and common sense in antagonism to faith is rationalism. The life of faith brings the two into right relationship. No one can solve the difficulty of making them one for me; I must do it for myself, and I can only solve it by life not by thinking, just as the natural can only be made spiritual in life, not in thinking. We have the idea that the body, individuality, and the natural life are altogether of the devil; they are not, they are of God, designed by God, and it is in the human body and in the natural order of things that we have to exhibit our worship of God. The danger is to mistake the natural for the spiritual, and instead of worshipping God in my natural life to make my natural life God.

How am I going to find out what the will of God is? In one way only, by not trying to find out. If you are born again of the Spirit of God, you *are* the will of God, and your ordinary common-sense decisions are God's will for you unless He gives an inner check. When He does, call a halt immediately and wait on Him. Be renewed in the spirit of your mind that you may make out His will, not in your mind, but in practical living. God's will in my common-sense life is not for me to *accept* conditions and say — 'Oh well, it is the will of God', but to *apprehend* them for Him, and that means conflict, and it is of God that we conflict. Doing the will of God is an active thing in my common-sense life.

### The Arbitration Between Abraham and Abimelech *(vv. 22–24)*

Abimelech does not stand for the sinful, but for the noble and upright and perfectly natural. The blessing of God is recognized by the natural, but never recognized by the sinful. Abimelech stands as the type of civilization with its organizations and culture and good sense. Between the church, which is an organism, and organization which is pagan, there must be arbitration. Much of our organization in the church is pagan, and it is our salvation to see that it is pagan. Immediately we forget this and compromise instead of arbitrate, we have sold the Son of God to the world. The attitude of faith to organization is illustrated in our Lord's attitude to Pilate. Our Lord did not compromise with Pilate, He arbitrated with him—'You have to decide this matter because God has put you in the position where you must. You stand there on your dignity as proconsul: I stand here on my dignity as Son of God. If you put me to death as your duty, I go to death because it is my duty.' There is no compromise there. 'If my kingdom *were* of this world, my servants would fight' (Jn 18:36); but there is no fight, there is arbitration, and the reason for it is God's order behind the whole thing.

## The Apprehension of Abimelech by Abraham

*(vv. 25–26)*

Abraham distinguishes clearly between political and private rights in this matter of the well, and now he in his turn administers a rebuke to Abimelech. In verse 26 Abimelech throws back the reproof on Abraham on the plea that he had not been told that the well had been taken away. This of course is mere natural shrewdness, and is the ground of their first arbitration. It is instructive to notice that Abraham always takes his rebukes magnificently; he never once shows individuality but always personality.

When first we become spiritual we arbitrate with our bodies until we say—I will put the natural into absolute subjection and have no more arbitration (see 1 Corinthians 9:27). The same kind of thing is taking place in the history of the world today. At present there is arbitration between the children of God and the natural forces of civilization. We arbitrate between the two by recognizing the present claims of each without compromising either. When the Lord Jesus comes again there will be no more arbitration; all the natural forces of civilization will instantly be put in subjection to Him, in the same way that those who enter into the sanctified life deliberately put the natural in themselves into subjection to Jesus Christ. In the meantime there is arbitration; no compromise and no fight, but deliberate arbitration between the two.

As Abimelech rebuked Abraham when he was in the wrong (see chapter 20), and Abraham in his turn rebuked Abimelech, so in the same way the children of men from time to time rebuke the children of God, and the children of God rebuke the politics of natural men. Compromise with each other or unity between them is immoral. Arbitration until He comes 'whose right it is to reign' is the God-ordained programme.

Abimelech exhibits the characteristic of natural, noble, worldly civilization which recognizes the blessing of God attached to the people of God, and shrewdly realizes the value of having the people of God in the midst of civilized life. No man on earth 'pooh-poohs' the people of God, although he himself does not intend to become one of them. Our Lord did not pray that His disciples should be taken out of the world, but that they should be kept from the evil one (Jn 17:15).

## The Agreement of Abraham and Abimelech

*(vv. 27–34)*

The Old Testament Scriptures always regard the oath as a peculiar sacrament. If you read what the Bible says about vowing you will see how culpably negligent we are in the way we promise. If we do not fulfil a promise, we damage our moral and spiritual life. It is infinitely better to refuse to promise anything, even in the most superficial relationships, than to promise and not perform. Spiritual leakages are accounted for in this way. Always do what you ought to do, but be careful of promising anything, because a promise puts the blood of God on your character. If you make a promise yu must see that it is fulfilled, no matter what it costs you. The glib way we promise is indicative of the slipshod ways we have got into, and of our laziness and indifference. The word of a natural man is his bond; the word of a saint binds God. It is a question of relationship to God all through.

The origin of the phrase 'business is business' is in the fact that business must not be carried on as a matter of faith but as a matter of covenant. Business is the go-between between the children of God and natural civilized life, and must be carried on by bonds.

By means of this arbitration Abraham's faith develops more fully into faith in the eternal truth of Jehovah's covenant (v. 33).

THIRTY

# THE SUPREME CLIMB

*Chapter 22:1–3*

Thy prayer shall be fulfilled; but how?
  His thoughts are not as thine,
While thou wouldst only weep and bow,
  He saih, 'Arise and shine!'
Thy thoughts were all of grief and night,
But His of boundless joy and light.
Thy Father reigns supreme above:
  Thy glory of His name
Is Grace and Wisdom, Truth and Love,
  His Will must be the same.
And thou hast asked all joys in one
In whispering forth, 'Thy will be done.'

*Frances Ridley Havergal*

Take...go to...offer on one of the mountains of which I shall tell you *(v. 2)*.

IN THE LIFE of Abraham we deal with the failures and the triumphs of the life of faith, and this chapter records the perfecting of the obedience of faith in Abraham. His obedience was not merely in the sacrifice of Isaac, but in his readiness to perceive a revelation even when it seemed to contradict what God had told him (cf. vv. 11–12). The very nature of faith is that it must be tried; faith untried is only ideally real, not actually real. Faith is not rational, therefore it cannot be worked out on the basis of logical reason; it can only be worked out on the implicit line by living obedience. God proves Abraham's faith by placing him in the most extreme crisis possible, because faith must prove itself by the inward concession of its dearest objects, and in this way be purified from all traditional and fanatical ideas and misconceptions.

## The Crucible for Abraham

God tested Abraham *(v. 1).*

The AV records, 'God did *tempt* Abraham.' Now these are startling words...the Holy Spirit caused it...God tempts no man (Jas 1:13). Again, our Lord taught us to pray 'do not lead us into temptation'; and He Himself was deliberately 'led up of the Spirit into the wilderness to be tempted of the devil'. The reason for the apparent contradiction is that there is a difference between the providence of God's rule and the providence of God's grace. The providence of God's grace is wrought out in the development of faith, and Paul refers to this when he says 'we know that all things work together for good to them that love God' — everything that happens transforms ideal faith into actual reality by the alchemy of God's providence (cf. Hebrews 12:11). The providence of God's grace is worked out in and through the arrangement of His rule, but is conditioned by the individual life of the one with whom He is dealing, e.g., God placed Abraham in a position He would not have placed Sarah or Lot. When we learn not to trust in our wits, we will never put ourselves where we have no business to be.

God does not further our spiritual life in spite of our circumstances, but in and by our circumstances. The whole purpose of God is to make the ideal faith actually real in the lives of His servants. God is working for His highest purpose until it and man's highest good become one.

God sits 'as a refiner and purifier of silver' – the crucible of testing is placed by God, not by man. It is easy to pass a crude verdict on God if you are not living in touch with Him. If you look at God through the mist of the heat of the crucible, you will say God is cruel. You must go through the crucible before you have any right to pronounce a verdict. On the off-side of the crucible a great many things are said which prove to be misconceptions – 'God took away my child because I loved her too much.' Go through the crucible, and you will find that in it you learned to know God better.

### The Concentration of Abraham

> Here I am *(v. 1)*.

These words express the greatest application of the human mind. To say 'Here I am' when God speaks is only possible if we are in His presence, in the place where we can obey. To understand where I am in the sight of God means not only to listen but to obey promptly all He says. I can always know where I am. Whenever I want to debate about doing what I know to be supremely right, I am not in touch with God.

### The Command to Abraham

> Take now your son, your only son Isaac, whom you love... *(v. 2)*.

God's words are, as it were, blows aimed against the incrustations of natural individual life in order that

Abraham's personal faith might be emancipated into fellowship with God. The blows are aimed at individuality because individuality will not come into fellowship with God; personality always does. Individuality is the husk of the personality, the home of independence and pride; but when God is developing the faith of a man all that must be sacrificed. It is the chrysalis developing into a butterfly, a winged creature of personal life. If you are not in the crucible yourself, the blows seem cruel; but if you are, you find the ecstasy of being brought into personal fellowship with God. Faith always works on the personal line (cf. Job 1:12).

God's command is — 'Take *now*…', not presently. To go to the height God shows can never be done presently, it must be done now. Every mother who gives her son in wartime climbs to the height instantly; There may be any amount of protest, but she climbs to the height and buries her son; her woman's heart goes through the bereavement long before it comes actually.

## The Climb for Abraham

> And offer him there as a burnt offering on one of the mountains of which I shall tell you *(v. 2).*

The mount of the Lord is the very height of the trial into which God brings His servant. There is no indication of the cost to Abraham; his implicit understanding of God so far outreaches his explicit knowledge that he trusts God utterly and climbs the highest height on which God can ever prove him, and remains unutterably true to God. There was no conflict — that was over; Abraham's confidence was fixed; He did not consult with flesh and blood, his own or anyone else's; he instantly obeyed. The point is that though all other voices should proclaim differently, obedience to the dictates of the Spirit of God at all costs is to be the attitude of the faithful soul. This mountain is not a mountain of sacrifice, but the mountain of proof that Abraham loved God supremely (see v. 12).

It is extraordinary how we debate with right. We know a thing is right but we try to seek excuses for not doing it now. Always beware when you want to confer with your own flesh and blood, i.e., your own sympathies, your own insight. These things are based on individuality, not on personal relationship to God, and they are the things that compete with God and hinder our faith. When our Lord is bringing us into personal relationship with Himself, it is always the individual relationships He breaks down. He comes with a sword rap on the husks that will not break, that will not let the life out for God (Mt. 10:34). 'If anyone comes to me and does not hate...he cannot be my disciple (Lk 14:26). If you are outside the crucible you will say that Jesus Christ is cruel, but when you are in the crucible you see that it is a personal relationship with Himself that He is after all the time. He is after the true gold, and the devil is after it too.

## The Consecration of Abraham

> So Abraham rose early in the morning...and went to the place of which God had told him *(v. 3)*.

Verse 3 reveals the wonderful simplicity of Abraham. This is the sacrifice of *Abraham*, not of Isaac. Always guard against self-chosen service for God; self-sacrifice may be a disease. God chose the crucible for Abraham, and Abraham made no demur, he went steadily through. If God has made your cup sweet, drink it with grace; if He has made it bitter, drink it in communion with Him. If it is a hard time of difficulty in the providential order of God, go through with it, but never choose your own service. If God has given the command, he will look after everything; your business is to get up and go, and smilingly wash your hands of the consequences.

Beware of pronouncing any verdict on the life of faith if you are not living it.

THIRTY-ONE

# ISOLATION

*Chapter 22:3–6*

Let no man think that sudden in a minute
  All is accomplished and the work is done;
Though with thine earliest dawn thou shouldst begin it,
  Scarce were it ended in thy setting sun.

How have I knelt with arms of my aspiring
  Lifted all night in irresponsive air,
Dazed and amazed with overmuch desiring,
  Blank with the utter agony of prayer!

*Myers*

The place afar off *(v. 4)*.

VERSE 1 STATES that God 'did tempt Abraham' (AV), and the context proves that the word 'tempt' has the underlying meaning of purifying; God had to lift Abraham's faith into an understanding of Himself. The life of Abraham is a life of faith, and faith in its actual working out has to go through spells of unsyllabled isolation (cf. Romans 8:26). Temptations in the life of faith are not accidents; each temptation is part of a plan, a step in the progress of faith. Faith is not logical, it works on the line of life and by its very nature must be tried. Never confound the trial of faith with the ordinary discipline of life. Much that we call the trial of our faith is the inevitable result of being alive. The problem lies in the clearing of God's character with regard to what

He allows. Faith according to the Bible is confidence in God when He is unscrutable and apparently contradictory in His providences.

## The Duty of Diligence

> So Abraham rose early in the morning *(v. 3)*.

This phrase is characteristic not only of men and women in the Bible, but of God Himself. The revelation of God in the Old Testament is that of a working God. No other religion presents God either as diligent or as suffering, but as an all-in-all principle, ruling in lofty disdain. The God who reveals Himself to Abraham is One ever intent on the fulfilment of His great designs; and like God, like people. If God is diligent, surely we ought to be diligent in doing our duty to Him. Think how patient and how diligent God has been with us! Over and over again God gets us near the point, and then by some petty individual sulk we spoil it all, and He patiently begins all over again. Think of the vision, 'whiter than snow shine', God gave of what He wanted us to be – where has it gone? Has God had to begin all over again from where we left off last time, or have we said – I will be true to God at all costs, no matter what the isolation?

## The Direction of Duty

> And went to the place of which God had told him *(v. 3)*.

Abraham took the direction of his duty from God's word, not from his own discernment (cf. Genesis 12:4; Hebrews 11:8). Our danger is to water down God's word to suit ourselves. God never fits His word to suit me; He fits me to suit His word. The discernment of God's call does not come in every moment of life, but only in rare moments; the moments our Lord spoke of as 'the light' (Jn 12:35–36). We have to remain true to what we see in those moments; if we do not, we will put back God's purpose in our life. The undercurrent of regret arises when we confer with those who have not heard the call of God, and if we listen to them we get into darkness. The life of Abraham is an illustration of two things: of unreserved surrender to God, and of God's complete possession of a child of His for His own highest ends.

It is never the consecration of our gifts that fits us for God's service. Profoundly speaking, we are not here to work for God. Absorption in practical work is one of the greatest hindrances in preventing a soul discerning the call of God. Unless active work is balanced by a deep isolated solitude with God, knowledge of God does not grow and the worker becomes exhausted and spent out. Our Lord said that the only men He will use in His enterprises are those in whom He has done everything (Lk 14:26, 27, 33); otherwise we would serve our own ends all the time. Many have begun well but have gone off on doctrine. All their energy is spent furthering a cause; Jesus Christ is not the dominating ruler. The direction of duty lies not in doing things for God, but in doing what God tells us to do, and God's order comes to us in the haphazard moments. We do not make the haphazard moments; God is the arranger of the haphazard. The direction of duty is loyalty to God in our present circumstances.

## The Discipline of Distance

Then on the third day... *(v. 4).*

God is never in a hurry. We say, 'I see what God wants and it seems so easy, I wish I could do it now.' Abraham had to travel many long hours to the place of sacrifice – a deed was to be done after days of reflection, not on the impulse of the moment – and during the journey not a look or a word betrayed his secret. Isaac never guessed at the isolation in his father's mind. Never reveal to anyone the profound depths of your isolation; when the life is going on profoundly with God, conceal it. 'Do not appear to men to be fasting.' It was this about our Lord that staggered the Pharisees; no one knew what He was going through in the profoundest concerns of His life. And at the end, when He might easily have been absorbed in the tremendous issue which He knew was at hand, He revealed no concern about Himself, only for His disciples – 'Let not your heart be troubled.'

## The Deception of Determination

The lad and I...will come back to you *(v. 5).*

The strength of Abraham's faith appears in that he held to God's promise while he promptly went to do what seemed to prevent its fulfilment. He believed that God would fulfil all He had promised and did not stay to question. To take God at His word may mean expecting God to come up to my standard; whereas true faith does not so much take God at His word as take the word of God as it is, in the face of all difficulties, and act upon it, with no attempt to explain or expound it.

## The Devotion of the Devoted

> So Abraham took the wood of the burnt offering, and laid it on Isaac his son *(v. 6).*

This verse is sublime. There is nothing more wonderful than the picture of this thoughtful, obedient boy going with his father, and even when he knew what the purpose was (v. 9), he was willing to relinquish the joy of life (cf. John 21:18).

THIRTY-TWO

# THE PATH OF GOD

## *Chapter 22:7–14*

My God, my God, let me for once look on thee
As though nought else existed, we alone!
And as creation crumbles, my soul's spark
Expands till I can say,—Even from myself
I need thee and I feel thee and I love thee.
I do not plead my rapture in thy works
For love of thee, nor that I feel as one
Who cannot die: but there is that in me
Which turns to thee, which loves or which should
  love.

*Browning*

God will provide for himself... *(v. 8).*

THE LIFE OF Abraham provides the pattern spiritual biography in which the life ascends from the rational and accountable to the personally traced footsteps of the soul's path to God. The turning points in the spiral ascent of faith are, first, obedience to the effectual call of God (ch. 12); and second, the culmination of unreserved resignation to God (ch. 22). Our difficulties spiritually arise from unrecognized spiritual hysterics, in which mood we unconsciously select God to watch us and our symptoms. The only cure for that is to get hold of God and have no symptoms.

## The Speech of Silent Spirituality *(vv. 7–8)*

The speech of Abraham and Isaac reveals that they are spiritually silent — the son is silent before the father as the father is silent before God, and thus God elevates them both above unspiritual human nature. That is, both father and son have gone one step beyond the limit of the possible because they are on the path of God. To talk easily about spiritual experiences is an indication that I have only a devout nodding acquaintance with the experiences of others, and am devoid of all such experiences myself.

In the life of faith the pressure of forethought is transferred to God by the faith which fulfils His behests; I have faith in God's accountable rationality, not in my own. If I have never heard the call of God; all I see is the accountability that I can state to myself. Practical work is nearly always a determination to think for myself, to take the pressure of forethought on myself; I see the need, therefore I must do something. That is not the effectual call of God, but the call of my sympathy with conditions as I see them. When God's call comes, I learn to do actively what He tells me and take no thought for the morrow. Take a step in faith in God, and your rational friends will say, 'Very beautiful, but suppose we all did it...!' You are not living on the line of accountable rationality, but a life of agreement with God's effectual call, and have therefore no reply to make.

In Hebrews 11:19 we get an insight into Abraham's spirituality — 'Accounting that God was able to raise him up, even from the dead.' It was not Abraham's common sense but his spiritual illumination that made him know it. Beware of turning a common-sense somersault and make God appear foolish by saying that Abraham knew all about it and it was not a sacrifice at all. Abraham did not know all about it; he believed that God would give Isaac back to him, but how, he had no notion. He surrendered himself entirely to the supernatural God. God never tells us what He is going to do, He reveals who He is.

'And the two of them went together' in the obedience of faith. Abraham stood in the midst of the most appalling personal controversy, the controversy between natural love and faith, and Isaac was worthy of his father. The path *to* God is never the same as the path *of* God. When I am going on with God in His path, I do not understand, but God does; therefore I understand God, not His path. When you take a step in faith in God and fulfil His behests, God does the forethinking for you. When you do it for yourself, God has to take second place. If you are going through the discipline of transferring your forethought to God and actively fulfilling His behests, you have to be silent; and when you do speak your speech is shallow – it does not convey where you are. People must never guess what you are going through. Piety always pretends to be going through what it is not.

### The Sacrifice of Surrendered Sonship *(vv. 9–10)*

God is the ruling factor in all our transactions (cf. Proverbs 20:24). When we commit ourselves to God He arranges the haphazard, and we have to see that we actively fulfil His behests where He places us.

The binding of Isaac is a prefiguring of the fulfilment and the perfection of the death of Christ. The emphasis of the so-called higher Christian life is to look at Christ as our Example, not as our sacrifice; by prayer and consecration we come into God's favour. We do not, that is blasphemy. God never accepts us because we obey; He can only accept us on the ground of sacrifice, which cost death. Therefore our approach to God can never be on the ground of our merit — that I am being bound by Another; that is the effect of the sacrifice of Christ in me. Personal holiness is never the ground of my acceptance with God; the only ground of acceptance is the death of the Lord Jesus Christ.

### THE SYMPATHY OF SUPREME SPIRIT *(vv. 11–12)*

Abraham had a rational understanding of what God's command meant and he had to step out of it. Abraham was not a fanatic; the instant the voice of God came he surrendered himself in devotion to the voice, although it seemed an arrest of obedience to the divine command. The essence of true religious faith is devotion to a Person. Beware of sticking to convictions instead of to Christ; convictions are simply the clothes of your growing life.

The great point of Abraham's faith in God was that he was prepared to do anything for God. Mark the difference between that and doing anything to *prove* your love to God. Abraham was there to obey God, no matter to what he went contrary. Abraham was not a pledged devotee of his own convictions, or he would have slain his son and said the voice of the angel was the voice of the devil. There is always the point of giving up convictions and traditional beliefs. If I will remain true to God, He will lead me straight through the ordeal into the inner chamber of a better knowledge of God. Our Lord taught us to pray 'lead us not into temptation.' Don't ask God to test you. Don't declare as Peter did, I will do anything, I will go to death for you. Abraham did not make any such declaration; he remained true to God, and God purified his faith.

Abraham is taught by the ancient ritual what Paul

clearly expressed in Romans 12:1. Verse 9 is a picture of the blunder of thinking that the sacrifice of death is the final thing God wants; what God wants is the sacrifice through death which enables a man to do what Jesus did, viz. sacrifice his life. Many of us think that God wants us to give up things; we make Christianity the great apotheosis of giving up! God purified Abraham from this blunder, and the same discipline goes on in our lives. 'Oh well, I expect God will ask me to give that up.' God nowhere tells us to give up things for the sake of giving them up; He tells us to give them up for the sake of the only thing worth having, viz. life with Himself. It is a question of loosening the bands that hinder our life, and immediately those bands are loosened by identification with the death of Jesus, we enter into a relationship with God whereby we sacrifice our life to God. To give God my life for death is of no value; what is of value is to let Him have all my powers that have been saved and sanctified, so that as Jesus sacrificed His life for His Father, I can sacrifice my life for Him. 'Present your bodies a *living* sacrifice,' says Paul.

### The Substitution of Sacramental Service

*(vv. 13–14)*

Abraham did not receive a positive command to sacrifice the ram; he recognized in the ram caught by his horns in a thicket behind him a divine suggestion. Until we get into fellowship with God His suggestions are no good to us. When people are intimate with one another suggestions convey more than words, and when God gets us into oneness with Himself we recognize His suggestions. Abraham offers the ram as a substitute for his son; he does not withhold his son in intention, although in fact he offers a substitute.

The entire system of sacrifice is an extention of the sacrifice of the ram. The spiritual sacrifice of Isaac and the physical sacrifice of the ram are made one; the natural and the spiritual are blended. That Christ is the substitute for me and therefore I go scot free, is never taught in the New Testament. If I say that Christ suffered instead of me, I knock the bottom board out of His sacrifice. *Christ died in the stead of me.* I, a guilty sinner, can never get right with God; it is impossible. I can only be brought into union with God by identification with the One who died in my stead. No sinner can get right with God on any other ground than the ground that Christ died *in his stead*, not *instead of him.*

THIRTY-THREE

# THE ETERNAL GOAL

## *Chapter 22:15–19*

My goal is God Himself, not joy, nor peace,
Nor even blessing, but Himself, my God;
'Tis His to lead me there, not mine, but His —
'At any cost, dear Lord, by any road!'

One thing I know, I cannot say Him nay;
One thing I do, I press towards my Lord;
My God my glory here, from day to day,
And in the glory there my Great Reward.

*F. Brook*

In blessing I will bless you . . . because you have obeyed my voice *(v. 17–18).*

THE SPIRIT of obedience gives more joy to God than anything else on earth. Obedience is impossible to us naturally; even when we do obey, we do it with a pout in our moral underlip, and with the determination to scale up high enough and then 'boss my boss'. In the spiritual domain there is no pout to be removed because the nature of God has come into me. The nature of God is exhibited in the life of our Lord, and the great characteristic of His life is obedience. When the love of God is shed abroad in my heart by the Holy Spirit (Rom. 5:5), I am possessed by the nature of God, and I show by my obedience that I love Him. The best measure of a spiritual life is not its ecstasies, but its obedience. 'To obey is better than sacrifice.'

### THE SUPREME CALL OF GOD *(v. 15)*

When God first called to Abraham there was still a dim gulf between them; God had to call and Abraham to answer (v. 1). Now that gulf is bridged. 'The angel of the Lord called a second time out of heaven...', i.e., an inward state of soul, and Abraham is so near to God that he does not need to reply; he is in the place of unimpeded listening. Is there any impediment between my ears and God's voice?

The call of God is a call in accordance with the nature of God, not in accordance with my idea of God. At first, Abraham did not interpret the call along the line of the nature of God because he did not know it; he interpreted it along the line of the Chaldaic tradition and took it to mean he was to kill his son. The supreme crisis in Abraham's faith has now been reached; all his imperfect conceptions of God have been left behind and he has come now to understand God. Always beware of self-assertiveness; it bruises our relationship to God, and distorts the manifestation of His nature in us. Abraham was neither an amateur providence nor a moral policeman; he simply believed God.

### THE SUPREME REALITY OF GOD *(v. 16)*

Abraham has come to the place where he is in touch with the very nature of God; he understands the reality of God, and God, as it were, unveils Himself to him in a burst of enthusiasm. There is no possibility of questioning on my part when God speaks, if He is speaking to His own nature in me; prompt obedience is the only result. When Jesus says 'Come to me,' I simply come; when He says 'Trust in God in this matter,' I do not try to trust, I *do* trust. An alteration has taken place in my disposition which is an evidence that the nature of God is at work in me.

## The Supreme Character of God *(vv. 17–18)*

The promise of God stands in relation to Abraham's tried and willing obedience. The revelation of God to me is determined by my character, not by God's (Ps. 18:25–26). If I am mean, that is how God will appear to me.

> 'Tis because I am mean, Thy ways so oft
> Look mean to me.

By the discipline of obedience, I come to the place Abraham reached and see God as He is. The promises of God are of no use to me until by obedience I understand the nature of God. We read some things in the Bible 365 times and they mean nothing to us, then all of a sudden we see what they mean, because in some particular we have obeyed God, and instantly His character is revealed. 'For all the promises of God in him are yes.' The 'yes' must be born of obedience; when by the obedience of our life, we say 'Amen', 'So let it be', to a promise, then that promise is made ours.

## The Supreme Reward *(v. 19)*

The more we have to sacrifice for God, the more glorious is the reward presently. We have no right to choose our sacrifice; God will let us see where the sacrifice is to come, and it will always be on the line of what God has given us, our 'Isaac', and yet His call is to sacrifice it. God is always at work on the principle of lifting up the natural and making it and the spiritual one, and very few of us will go through with it. We will cling to the natural when God wants to put a sword through it. If you go through the transfiguration of the natural, you will receive it back on a new plane altogether. God wants to make eternally our own what we only possessed intermittently.

In the beginning we do not train for God, we train for work, for our own aims, but as we go on with God we lose all our own aims and are trained into God's purpose. Unless practical work is appointed by God, it will prove a curse (cf. John 17:18). 'At any cost, by any road,' means nothing self-chosen. The Bible does not say that God blessed Abraham and took him to heaven; but that He blessed him and kept him on earth. The maturity of character before God is the personal channel through which He can bless others. If it takes all our lifetime before God can put us right, then others are going to be impoverished. We need to hurry and climb our Mount Moriah, come to the place where God can put an end to the dim gulf between Him and ourselves, then He will be able to bless us as He did Abraham.

No language can express the ineffable blessedness of the supreme reward that awaits the soul that has taken its supreme climb, proved its supreme love, and entered on its supreme reward. What an imperturbable certainty there is about the man who is in contact with the real God! Thank God, the life of the Father of the Faithful is but a specimen of the life of every humble believer who obediently follows the discipline of the life of faith. What a depth of transparent rightness there must be about the man who walks before God, and the meaning of the Atonement is to place us there in perfect adjustment to God. 'Walk before me, and be blameless', not faultless, but blameless, undeserving of censure in the eyes of God.

THIRTY-FOUR

# STILL HUMAN

*Chapter 22:20–24*

For some may follow truth from dawn to dark
As a child follows by his mother's hand,
Knowing no fear, rejoicing all the way;
And unto some her face is as a star
Set through an avenue of thorns and fires,
And waving branches, black without a leaf.

And still it draws them, though the feet must bleed,
Though the garments must be rent and eyes be
  scorched;
And if the valley of the shadow of death
Be passed, and to the level road they come,
Still with their faces to the polar star,
It is not with the same looks, the same limbs,
But halt and maimed and of infirmity.

Now it came to pass...that it was told Abraham *(v. 20).*

## God's Omniscience and Human Life

What the natural reason would call an anticlimax is the very climax of God's supernatural grace whereby a man having gone through the most wonderful experience, emerges and lives an unwonderful, ordinary life. That is the difference between the fanatic and the faithful soul. You find it all through the New Testament. The wonder of the Incarnation slips into the life of ordinary childhood; the marvel of the Transfiguration descends to the valley and the demon-possessed boy, and the glory of the Resurrection merges into our Lord providing breakfast for His disciples on the sea shore in the early dawn. The tendency in early Christian experience is to look for the marvellous. We are apt to mistake the sense of the heroic for being heroes. It is one thing to go through a crisis grandly, but a different thing to go through every day glorifying God when there is no witness, no limelight, and no one paying the remotest attention to you. If we don't want medieval haloes, we want something that will make people say — What a wonderful man of prayer he is! What a pious, devoted woman she is! If anyone says that of you, you have not been loyal to God. If you are rightly devoted to Jesus Christ, you have reached the sublime height where no one thinks of noticing you; all that is noticed is that the power of God comes through all the time. It is along some such line as this that we are to understand the omniscience of God and human life. 'Oh, I have had a wonderful call from God!' It takes Almighty God Incarnate in you to peel potatoes properly, and to wash heathen children for the glory of God. *Anyone* cannot do these things; anybody can do the shining in the sun and the sporting in the footlights, but it takes God's incarnated Spirit to make you so absolutely humanly His that you are utterly unnoticeable.

## God's Object and Human Nature

The history of the life of Abraham does not close abruptly with his greatest act of faith, but from that act of faith there is a natural human progress to a sanctified life. Human nature likes to read about the heroic and the intense: it takes the divine nature to be interested in grass and sparrows and trees, because they are so unutterably commonplace, and also because God happens to have made them. God's order is the human; the devil's is the spectacular. The object of the crisis is that we may live the human life in perfect relation to God.

Abraham is not the type of a saint or of sanctification, but of the life of faith. Our human relationships are the actual conditions in which the ideal life of God is to be exhibited. Any sordid being can sit in a cathedral in the twilight and listen to beautiful music and feel divine; Abraham lived as God's man in the earthly conditions of his life. If the indwelling of God cannot be manifested in human flesh, then the Incarnation and the Atonement are of no avail. All our Christian work may be merely scaffolding poles to prepare us so that God may do what He likes with us, unobtrusively. The test of the life of a saint is not success, but faithfulness as a steward of the mysteries of God in human life as it actually is (cf. Luke 6:40). We will put up success as the aim in Christian work; the one thing glorifying to God is the glory of God manifested in human lives unobtrusively. The 'show business' belongs to the pagan order of things; devotion to God in actual human conditions belongs to the redemptive order. A Christian is one who has learned to live the life hid with Christ in God in human conditions.

### God's Order and Human Haphazard *(v. 20)*

The message which Abraham received was providential and came at the right moment. The message was apparently haphazard, but it was all in the order of God. It is a great moment in the life of a child of God when letters and messages are seen to be under the direction of divine providence. When God brings me a word on occasions and I obey it, He will look after everything else. There is nothing haphazard to a child of God (Rom. 8:28).

## God's Opportunity and Human Forethought

*(vv. 21–23)*

Abraham must soon think of Isaac's marriage, and the message from his kindred causes him to hope that he may find in his brother's family a bride for Isaac. Remain true to God in your obscurity, and remember you are not the designer of your destiny. You hear the call of God and realize what He wants, then you begin to find reasons why you should not obey Him. Well, obey Him, because away in some other part of the world there are other circumstances being worked by God, and if you say – 'I shan't, I wasn't made for this,' you get out of touch with God. Your 'goings' are not according to your mind, but according to God's mind. Remain true at all costs to what God is doing with you and don't ask why He is doing it. Don't loaf along like a strayed poet on the fringes of God's providence; the Almighty has got you in hand. Leave yourself alone and trust in Him. Half the sentimental pious folks that strew the coasts of emotional religious life are there because we will engineer our own circumstances. We have to be for God's purpose, and God cannot explain His purpose until it happens. God's omniscience, God's order, and God's opportunity in my individual life all work together, and Jesus Christ enters into my life just at the point of the haphazard circumstances I am in. Sanctification is not the end of Redemption; it is the gateway to the purpose of God. No Christian experience is the end and purpose of Redemption. God's own plans are the purpose of Redemption.

When the call of Jesus Christ comes, it comes to *you*. It cannot come to your father or your mother, or to your wife, or to your own self-interest; it comes entirely to your personal life. Instantly the clamour begins. Father and mother say no, the claims of my own life say no; Jesus Christ says yes. Think — could Jesus Christ's call mean that I hurt my father and mother irrevocably? Certainly it could not; then if I obey Him, even though it looks like bringing the sword and the upset into lives, in the final wind up God will bring His wisdom out perfectly, and I shall find that every one of those human relationships have been brought in in the wake of my obedience. The point is — will I trust God, or lean to my own convictions? Obedience to the supremacy of the Lord Jesus is the only legitimate outcome of sanctification. Thank God, He wants us to be human, not spooks!

THIRTY-FIVE

# HUMAN GREATNESS

## *Chapter 23*

We cannot kindle when we will
  The fire which in the heart resides;
The spirit bloweth and is still,
  In mystery our soul abides.
    But tasks in hours of insight will'd
    Can be through hours of gloom fulfill'd.

With aching hands and bleeding feet,
  We dig and heap, lay stone on stone;
We bear the burden and the heat
  Of the long day, and wish 'twere done.
    Not till the hours of light return
    All we have built do we discern.

*Matthew Arnold*

You are a prince of God (a mighty prince) *(v. 6)*.

### In the Place of Sorrow *(vv. 1–2)*

The Old Testament relates the end of no other woman's life so particularly as it does the end of Sarah's life. Abraham's personal sorrow is recorded in the words – 'to weep for her'. It is a farce to make nothing of death; the natural expressions of the heart are not suppressed, but tempered and transfigured. It is no part of faith to affect insensibility to sorrow; that is stoical humbug. In certain stages of religious experience we have the idea that we must not show sorrow when we are sorrowful. That idea is an enemy to the Spirit of Jesus Christ, because it leads to heartlessness and hypocrisy. Not to sorrow is not even human; it is diabolical. The Spirit of God hallows sorrow.

In dealing with the life of Abraham as the Father of the Faithful neither faith nor common sense must be our guide, but God who unites both in the alchemy of personal experience. To be guided by common sense alone is fanatical; both common sense and faith have to be brought into relation to God. The life of faith does not consist of acts of worship or of great self-denial and heroic virtues, but of all the daily conscious acts of our lives.

## In the Place of Sojourning *(vv. 3–4)*

The phrase Abraham uses, 'a stranger and sojourner', is the inner meaning of the term 'Hebrew'. Abraham could never say that he was at home in Canaan; he left his home never to find another on earth. The thought of pilgrimage sank deep into the Hebrew mind, and the note of the sojourner is essentially the note of the Christian. Instead of being pilgrims and strangers on the earth, we become citizens of this order of things and entrench ourselves here, and the statements of Jesus have no meaning. The genius of the Spirit of God is to make us pilgrims, consequently there is the continual un-at-home-ness in this world (cf. Philippians 3:20). It is a matter of indifference to the Spirit of God where we are, and it ought to be equally indifferent to us. As saints, we are cursed, not blessed, by patriotism. The idea of nations is man's, not God's. When our Lord establishes His kingdom there will be no nations, only the great kingdom of God. That is why His kingdom is not built up on civilized life.

### In the Place of Sentiment *(vv. 8–9)*

Sentiment is thought occasioned by feeling; sentimentality is feeling occasioned by thought. Sentiment plays an important part in human affairs, and no sentiment is more sacred than that connected with our dead. Sentimentality is produced by watching things we are not in. Go through a disaster or bereavement, and the emotions produced are the bedrock of feeling which makes human life worthy. As Christians we should conduct our lives on the high sentiment which is the outcome of a transaction with the Lord Jesus Christ. If our testimony is hard, it is because we have gone through no crisis with God; there is no heart-broken emotion behind it. If we have been through a crisis in which human feeling has been ploughed to its inner centre by the Lord, our testimony will convey all the weight of the greatness of God along with human greatness. It is essential to go through a crisis with God which costs you something, otherwise your devotional life is not worth anything. You cannot be profoundly moved by nothing, or by doctrine; you can only be profoundly moved by devotion.

Verses 8 to 9. The story of Abraham's palaver with the Hittites conveys the idea that they had respect for the true greatness of Abraham.

> Bending before men is a recognition that there does dwell in that presence of our brother something divine.
>
> *Carlyle*

We all recognize human trappings; only one in a thousand recognizes human greatness. We bow not to greatness, but to the trappings of money and of birth. If I bow because I must, I am a conventional fraud; if I bow because I recognize true greatness, it is a sign that I am being emancipated. The greatest humiliation for a Christian is to recognize that he has ignored true greatness because it was without trappings. If the Pharisees had been reverent towards true greatness, they would not have treated the Nazarene carpenter as they did.

## In the Place of Scrupulosity *(vv. 17–18)*

The details of this palaver must not be passed over. We are apt to say that religion is religion, and business is business; but there is no cleavage in the life of faith. Slovenliness is an insult to the Holy Spirit. Our Lord is scrupulous in His saving of us; surely we can be scrupulous in the conduct of His temple, our bodies and our bodily connections. That will mean God's greatness coming down into our human setting, and we see to it that we do everything in keeping with the greatness of God.

## In the Place of Sublimity *(v. 6)*

The Hittites had no word for 'gentleman', so they called Abraham 'a prince of God'. Abraham kept company with God until he became a partaker of the divine nature. It is impossible for a saint, no matter what his experience, to keep right with God if he will not take the trouble to spend time with God. In order to keep the mind and heart awake to God's high ideals you have to keep coming back again and again to the primal source. If you do not, you will be crushed into degeneracy. Just as a poet or an artist must keep his soul brooding on the right lines, so a Christian must keep the sense of God's call always awake. Spend plenty of time with God; let other things go, but don't neglect Him. And beware of practical work. We are not here to do work *for* God, we are here to be workers *with* Him, those through whom He can do His work.

THIRTY-SIX

# BEATIFIC BETROTHAL

## *Chapter 24*

War and Woof and Tangle, —
*Weavers of Webs are we.*
Living and dying — and mightier dead,
For the shuttle, once sped, is sped — is sped; —
*Weavers of Webs are we.*

White, and Black, and Hodden-gray, —
*Weavers of Webs are we.*
To every weaver one golden strand
Is given in trust by the Master-Hand; —
*Weavers of Webs are we.*

And that we weave, we know not, —
*Weavers of Webs are we.*
The threads we see, but the pattern is known
To the Master-Weaver alone, alone; —
*Weavers of Webs are we.*

*John Oxenham*

Come in, blessed of the Lord! Why do you stand outside? *(v. 31).*

NOTHING CAN exceed the dignity and beauty of this chapter in the Bible. It reveals God's providential workings in the lives of several elemental, upright people, and clearly conveys God's order for each one. In the case of Abraham we see sublime sentiment (thought born in profound feeling) being worked out in plain common-sense details, yet with the natural sensibilities alive at once to human conditions and to the demands of God.

## Sentiment, Sense and Sensibility

As already stated, there is a difference between sentiment and sentimentality. We cannot be profoundly moved by thought; we can only be profoundly moved by a personal crisis with God in which our usual equilibrium is disturbed, and our subsequent conceptions of life must be taken from the emotions stirred by the crisis. If the disturbance comes to you from outside, you will be exactly the same after it; but if you go through a personal crisis, such as our Lord insists on, the personal crisis of devotion to Himself in discipleship, then all your conceptions of life will take colour from that moment. People are called backsliders who are merely sentimental pious people. They have had no crisis; all they have is the affectation of sentimentality. Recall the depths of feeling through which God has taken Abraham, and now in this chapter we see him being led rightly in the actual concerns of life. Right views on profound subjects will always be the spring of right relationships in shallow matters. To be guided by common sense is as foolish as being guided by faith. God is the One who welds both faith and common sense into one practical personality.

By 'sense' understand matters of practical human existence, and remember that any feature of actual life not brought under the severe control of the conception born of your crisis with God will leave a loophole for the devil. For instance, if you ignore certain aspects of your natural life as it has been constructed by God – take too much sleep, or not enough sleep, forego meals – you will give occasion to the enemy straightaway, no matter how great a saint you are. We have no business to leave out any part of our being from the control of the conceptions born of our crisis with God. The difficulty with us as Christians is that we will not think in accordance with the crisis we have had; consequently when we come to the things of sense and meet with people who have not had a crisis with God, it is an easy business to climb down. If we remain true to the sentiment produced in us by our crisis with God, those who meantime protest against us will ultimately come up to the same standard; but if we succumb, everything will go down.

By 'sensibility' understand the natural intuitive power usually called tact, which makes it possible for us to live with other people without annoying them. These three — sentiment, sense and sensibility — must be welded into one in our personal lives by devotion to the Lord Jesus Christ.

## Solemn Sacredness of Serving

Eliezer in many respects stands as a picture of a disciple of the Lord; the whole moulding of his life is his devotion to another, not to a sense of right or duty, but to his master (cf. John 13:13–14). We know very little about devotion to Jesus Christ. We know about devotion to right and to duty, but none of that is saintly; it is purely natural. My sense of duty and of right can never be God's. If I can state what my duty is, I have become my god in that particular. There is only One who knows what my duty is as a Christian, and that is God. The Sermon on the Mount nowhere tells us what our duty is; it tells us the things a saint will do — things that are not his duty, e.g., Matthew 5:39–42. Be renewed in the spirit of your mind, says Paul, not that you may do your duty, but that you may make out what God's will is.

All the reward Eliezer seeks is the happiness of his master; self-remembrance in him is dead. He is shrewd and practical, yet as guileless as a child, the exact embodiment of 1 Corinthians 4:2—'It is required in stewards, that a man be found *faithful.*'

## Self-forgetfulness in Stewards of Secrets

One significant thing to notice is that Rebecca came alone and unveiled, and conversed freely with a stranger. The self-forgetfulness of Eliezer and Rebecca's own intuition made her know that she was safe with him. 'Man's virtue and woman's liberty go hand in hand.' There are those who talk like angels, yet they smudge the soul; there are others who may not talk sweetly yet they exhilarate the soul. Guard your intuition as the gift of God. You cannot judge virtue by its obverse; you can only judge virtue by intuition. Woe be to any woman who ignores her intuition, ignores the warning which says—Now draw back. For God's sake and your own womanhood's sake, draw back, it matters not who the person is.

## Sweet Supremacy of Singleness

Rebecca's brother and mother recognize God's hand in the whole matter (v. 50), and Rebecca's consent is sought only on the point of departure. 'And she said, I will go.' Those words are the answer to Eliezer's prayer. Rebecca felt the thrill which always passes through any pure young heart in the presence of a saint. A soul's trust in a saint in the providence of God is something more precious even than love. Few of us know anything about it because we are too sordidly selfish; we want things for ourselves all the time. Eliezer had only one conception — loyalty to his master — and in the providence of God he brought Rebecca straight to Isaac. This marriage, like all true marriages, concerns the kingdom of God.

THIRTY-SEVEN

# DISCOVERING DIVINE DESIGNS

## *Chapter 24*

Let us not always say
'Spite of this flesh to-day
I strove, made head, gained ground upon the whole!'
As the bird wings and sings,
Let us cry 'All good things
Are ours, nor soul helps flesh more, now, than flesh helps soul!'

He fixed thee mid this dance
Of plastic circumstance,
This Present, thou, forsooth, wouldst fain arrest:
Machinery just meant
To give thy soul its bent,
Try thee and turn thee forth, sufficiently impressed.

*Browning*

Then the man bowed down his head and worshipped the Lord *(v. 26)*.

THE WHOLE discipline of the life of faith is to make the ideal visions of faith and the actual performance of life one in personal possession. Only one Being can enable us to make the ideal and the actual one in personal life, viz., the Holy Spirit. In art and literature the ideal and the actual are only made one in a picture or a poem or book. The temple of the Holy Spirit is our personal life.

## Human Forethought and Divine Design *(vv. 1–9)*

Abraham's motive is clearly stated here. Never speak of human motives as if they were opposed to the divine. In the life of a child of God the human motive is the disguised divine. Sanctification means that I become a child of God, consequently my common-sense decisions are God's will unless He gives the check of His Spirit. I decide things in perfect fellowship with God, knowing that if my decisions are wrong, He will check. When He checks, I must stop at once. It is the inner check of the Spirit that prevents common sense being our god. There are times of crisis when we must wait on God, but they are rare. It is the abortion of piety to ask God to guide us here and there. Of course He will! Such asking is not real. Remember our Lord's injunction – 'Unless you become as little children.'

If God is not recognized by His blessings in the details of actual life in the beginning, He will be recognized in the end by His destructions. Human forethought in a faithful soul such as Abraham is the manifestation of the divine design. In looking back you see not the haphazard, but an amazing design which, if you are born of God, you will credit to God; otherwise you credit it to the extraordinary wisdom of men and women.

## Human Appointments and Divine Discoveries *(vv. 10–21)*

It is our wisdom to follow providence, but folly to force it. By earnest human effort Eliezer makes his appointments, and these are not only recognized by God, but become also discoveries of the divine mind. Unless you are a saint, your praying is pious humbug;

but if you are a saint, you soon realize that you discover the divine by energetically doing the human, provided you are maintaining a personal relationship to God. The fanatical element in the saint is the element that is devoted to a principle instead of to consistent conduct before God. For instance, I may become a devotee to the doctrine of divine healing which means I must never be sick, and if I am sick then I say I must have gone wrong. The battle all through is against the absurdity of being consistent to an ideal instead of to God. The vital point about Eliezer is not his asking for signs, but that *Eliezer* asked for signs. Eliezer was a man who related everything entirely to God, consequently his human appointments, which are easy to ridicule, were God's way of enabling him to discover His mind. Beware of making a fetish of consistency to convictions instead of developing your faith in God. 'I shall never do that' — in all probability you will have to if you are a saint. Whenever we take what God has done and put it in the place of Himself, we instantly become idolaters. If our Lord had been fanatically consistent, He would have said after the temptation — I have not eaten for forty days, therefore I will never eat food again. He did not eat for forty days because it was His Father's will for Him not to. Judged on the line of logical consistency there was no more inconsistent being than our Lord. He said — 'Do not resist evil'; and then He cleansed the temple in Jerusalem. (Mk 11:15–16). But our Lord was never inconsistent to His Father. The saint is to be consistent to the divine life within him, not logically consistent to a principle. A fanatic is concerned not about God but about proving his own little fanatical ideas. It is a danger peculiar to us all. It is easier to be a fanatic than a faithful soul, because there is something amazingly humbling, particularly to our religious conceit, in being loyal to God.

## Human Astonishment and Divine Details
*(vv. 22–33)*

The details of these verses are commonplace to Eastern custom, but Eliezer sees God in them. It is easy to see God in exceptional things or in a crisis, but it requires the culture of spiritual discipline to see God in every detail. Never allow that the haphazard is anything less than God's appointed order.

One other thing to note in these verses is the characteristic of the hospitality—it is an incurious, generous hospitality, which is the rarest type. Hospitality is characteristic not only of the East but of God's programme. To be curious about another person's affairs is an impertinence and is never Christian.

## Human Affinities and Divine Directions
*(vv. 34–49)*

Eliezer gives a simple account of his journey, but his speech is an example of great wisdom. When the Spirit of God guides a man's human affairs, his speech indicates not human shrewdness, but the frankness of divine skill. Always note that we must be ready to discover the divine designs *anywhere*.

## Human Abandon and Divine Devotion
*(vv. 50–67)*

The custom according to which the brother must interest himself in the affairs of the sister is the explanation of much in these verses. They recognized the will of God in the whole matter, and have neither good nor ill to say. The consent of Rebecca is not sought in the betrothal, but only in the less important point of immediate departure.

When a soul abandons to God, God will not abandon it. But let that soul trust its wits and become its own amateur providence and a dexterous muddle will be the result. When once you have the amateur providence idea, it will prevent your doing the thing God tells you to do — 'I must not tell my parents about my call; I want to prevent them suffering.' Your plain duty before God is to tell them. If you are abandoned to God and do the duty that lies nearest, God will not abandon you; but if you trust in your wits and bring in the amateur providence idea, He will have to abandon you, and there will be heartbreaks and distresses that he is not in at all. Present the whole thing where it ought to be presented — in abandonment to God, and He will engineer everything in His own way.

THIRTY-EIGHT

# SUNSET

## *Chapter 25:1–10*

That low man seeks a little thing to do,
    Sees it and does it:
This high man, with a great thing to pursue,
    Dies ere he know it.
That low man goes on adding one to one,
    His hundred's soon hit:
This high man, aiming at a million,
    Misses an unit.
That, has the world here – should he need the next,
    Let the world mind him!
This, throws himself on God, and unperplexed,
    Seeking shall find him.

*Browning*

And his sons Isaac and Ishmael buried him *(v. 9)*.

IT IS NOT what a man achieves, but what he believes and strives for that makes him noble and great. Hebrews 11 impresses this aspect of the life of faith over against the life of human perfection. The first thing faith in God does is to remove all thought of relevant perfection. Some lives may seem humanly perfect and yet not be relevant to God and His purpose. The effect such lives leave is not of a reach that exceeds its grasp, but of a completed little circle of their own. It takes a man completely severed from God to be perfect in that way. There is a difference between a perfect human life lived on earth and a personal life with God lived on earth; the former grasps that for which it reaches, the latter is grasped by that which it never can reach. The former chains us to earth by its very completeness, the latter causes us to fling ourselves unperplexed on God. The difference is not a question of sin, but the paradox of the incomplete perfection of a right relationship to God.

### The Region of the Irrelevant *(vv. 1–4)*

One of the most striking features in Abraham's life is its irrelevancy. If we take Abraham to be the embodiment of an idea, say, of sanctification, we will have to cut out much that God puts in. The irrelevant things in Abraham's life are evidences of that half-unconscious living which proves that his mind was not taken up with himself. The greatest thing in Abraham's life is God, not 'Abraham-ism'. The whole trend of his life is to make us admire God, not Abraham.

The outstanding characteristic in the life of a saint is its irrelevance, an irrelevance which is amazingly relevant to the purpose of God. If you become a devotee to a principle, you become a religious lunatic; you are no longer loyal to the life of Jesus, but loyal only to the logic of your convictions about Him. A fanatic dismisses all irrelevancy in life. We say that a lunatic is a man wh has lost his reason; a lunatic is a man who has lost everything but his reason. A madman's explanation of things is always complete. The main thing is life, not logic. It is the irrelevant running all through life that makes it what it is worth.

One of the dangers of the so-called higher Christian life movements is the idea that God wants to produce specimens to put in His museum. You can often find better specimens in the world than in the church.

Think of the men and women you know who have not been through the crisis you have been through, and your human reason tells you they are infinitely better than you are; they are more unselfish, never irritable or upset, and yet they would not dream of saying what you have to say, that you are loyal to Jesus Christ. The irrelevancy of your life and the relevancy of theirs will produce perplexity in your mind until you remember that you are not called to produce one of God's specimens; you are called to live in perfect relationship to God so that the net result of your life is not admiration for you, but a longing after God. Christian perfection is not, and never can be, human perfection. Christian perfection is the perfection of a relationship to God which shows itself in the total irrelevancy of human life.

If you get off on the line of personal holiness or divine healing or the Second Coming of our Lord, and make any of these your end, you are disloyal to Jesus Christ. Supposing the Lord has healed your body and you make divine healing your end; the dead set of your life is no longer for God but for what you are pleased to call the manifestation of God in your life. Bother your life! 'It can never be God's will that I should be sick.' If it was God's will to bruise His own Son, why should it not be His will to bruise you? The thing that tells is not relevant consistency to an idea of what a saint's life is, but abandonment abjectly to Jesus Christ whether you are well or ill.

Much of our life is irrelevant to any and every mind saving God's mind. When you obey the call of God the first thing that strikes you is the irrelevancy of the things you have to do, and you are sure to be brought up full butt against the perfect human specimens. The net result of such lives does not leave you with the 'flavour' of God at all; it leaves you with the idea that

God is totally unnecessary—by human effort and human devotion we can reach the standard God wants. Well, in a fallen world it cannot be done. Paul refers to this in 2 Corinthians 4:3–4—'the god of this age has blinded the minds of those who do not believe...', i.e., they have the perfection of the human, but never once have they seen the perfection of God.

Beware of taking your conception of a saint from deductions from certain Scriptures, and always clarify your views by meditation on John 17. God wants to do with the saints what His Son prayed He would do—make them one with Himself (v. 21).

### The Reign of the Irrevocable *(vv. 5–7)*

Ishmael is the son born of the wrong way of doing God's will. If we try to do God's will through our own effort, we produce Ishmael. Much of our modern Christian enterprise is 'Ishmael', i.e., it is born not of God, but of an inordinate desire to do God's will in our own way—the one thing our Lord never did.

Ishmael, as we have seen, had to be dismissed and disciplined until he was willing to become subservient and be utilized for God's purposes; and the natural has to be put completely under, dismissed and denied, until it is willing to be subjected to God, not to our ideas of relevancy. We put sin in the wrong place. Remember, we cannot touch sin. We must not tamper with it for one second. We can do nothing with sin; we must leave God's Redemption to deal with it. Our part has to do with 'Ishmael', i.e., the natural. The natural has to be denied, not because it is bad and wrong, but because it has nothing to do with our life of faith in God until it is turned into the spiritual by obedience. It is the attitude of the maimed life, which so few of us understand.

### The Realm of the Irreproachable *(v. 8)*

The Hebrews regarded life as complete when it was full of days and riches and honour. Age was looked upon as a sign of favour. Whenever a nation becomes unspiritual, it reverses this order; the demand is not for old age but for youth. This reversal in the modern life of today is indicative of apostasy, not of advance.

Abraham's life wore to a tranquil sunset. He is described as 'full of years', i.e., satisfied with life. He had seen, felt, believed, loved, suffered enough; earth had no more to offer him. Through God's goodness he found goodness in everything. Bitterness and cynicism are born of broken gods; bitterness is an indication that somewhere in my life I have belittled the true God and made a god of human perfection.

### The Reunion of the Irreconcilable *(vv. 9–10)*

Ishmael and Isaac are reunited at the grave of their father. Ishmael – strong, rugged, human perfection; Isaac – meditative, incomplete visionary, but on the trail of God. These two unite at the burial of Abraham, the Friend of God, whom God will not forsake. 'Gathered to his people' means gathered to the unseen world. This is immortality in direct statement in the Old Testament.

THIRTY-NINE

# ABIDING FACTORS

*Chapter 26:1–12*

## COMMENCEMENT OF DESTITUTION

> There was a famine in the land, besides the first famine that was in the days of Abraham *(v. 1).*

ISAAC'S HISTORY commences with the same trial as Abraham's, viz., a famine in the land. Abraham acted according to his own wits, not according to his faith in God: 'and Abram went down to Egypt to sojourn there; for the famine was severe in the land' — destitution in the very land of promise. Watch the destitution of wits that follows quickly on the heels of a divine revelation. Whenever you get a revelation from God you will be starved at once, starved, that is, in your wits — you can see no way out. Every time your wits compete with the worship of God you had better take a strong dose of Isaiah 30:15–16 — 'In returning and rest you shall be saved; in quietness and confidence shall be your strength. But you would not.' Beware of restlessness and wits persuading you that God has made a blunder — 'God would never allow me to fall sick after giving me such a blessing'; but He has! No matter what revelations God has made to you, there will be destitution so far as the physical apprehension of things is concerned — God gives you a revelation that He will provide, then He provides nothing and you begin to realize that there is a famine, of food, or of clothes, or money, and your common sense as well as other people's says, 'Abandon your faith in God, do this, and that.' Do it at your peril. Watch where destitution comes; if it comes on the heels of a time of quiet confidence in God, then thank Him for it and stay starving and He will bring a glorious issue.

## Command in Trial

> Then the Lord appeared to him and said: Do not go down to Egypt; dwell in the land of which I shall tell you *(v. 2)*.

The command to Abraham was to depart; the command to Isaac is to remain. When the 'Isaac' life of quietness and confidence in God is born of the 'Abraham' life of strenuous separation, don't make any more separations; just be still, and know that God is God. Those who educate you in the things of God will be the first to pull you back when you obey the voice which came through them. God taught you the right thing through them, and now you are obeying they come in with their own wits and say, 'Of course we didn't mean you should do that'; but God did. Beware of mixing quietness and confidence with other people's wits.

## Confirmation of Truth *(vv. 3–5)*

> ...because Abraham obeyed my voice, and kept my charge, my commandments, my statutes and my laws *(v. 5)*.

Isaac is promised divine blessing and protection because of God's oath which He swore to Abraham on account of his obedience. Abraham's obedience was far from perfect, but its great characteristic was its unreservedness. Abandon in the profound sense is of infinitely more value than personal holiness. Personal holiness brings the attention to bear on my own whiteness; I dare not be indiscreet, or unreserved, I dare not do anything in case I incur a speck. God can't bless that sort of thing; it is as unlike His own character as could be. The holiness produced through the indwelling of His Son in me is a holiness which is never conscious of itself. There are some people in whom you cannot find a speck and yet they are not abundantly blessed of God, while others make grave indiscretions and get marvellously blessed; the reason being that the former have become devotees of personal holiness, conscientious to a degree; the latter are marked by abandonment to God. Whatever centres attention on anything other than our Lord Himself will always lead astray. The only way to be kept cleansed is by walking in the light, as God is in the light. Only as we walk in that light is the holiness of Jesus Christ not only imputed, but imparted, to us.

Abraham's aberrations sprang not from disobedience, but from trusting in his own wits. Directly God's command was made known to him, he obeyed; when there was no command he was inclined to trust in his wits, and that is where he went wrong. It is never right to do wrong in order that right may come, although it may seem justifiable from every standard saving one. In the long run you can never produce right by doing wrong, yet we will always try to do it unless we believe what the Bible says. If I tell a lie in order to bring about the right, I prove to my own conviction that I do not believe the One at the back of the universe is truthful. Judge everything in the light of Jesus Christ, who is the Truth, and you will never do the wrong thing however right it looks.

FORTY

# THE TENDER GRACE

*Chapter 26:13–25*

THE ONLY RIGHT a Christian has is the right to give up his rights. This is the tender grace which is usually looked upon as an exhibition of lack of gumption. The embarrassing thing about Christian graces is that immediately you imitate them they become nauseating, because conscious imitation implies an affected preference for certain qualities, and we produce frauds by a spurious piety. All the qualities of a godly life are characteristic of the life of God. You cannot imitate the life of God unless you have it; then the imitation is not conscious, but the unconscious manifestation of the real thing. 'Pi' people try to produce the life of God by sheer imitation; they pretend to be sweet when really they are bitter. The life of God has no pretence, and when His life is in you, you do not pretend to feel sweet, you *are* sweet.

## THE EXTERNAL GREATNESS OF ISAAC

> The man began to prosper, and continued prospering until he became very prosperous *(v. 13).*

Isaac never became great in the way that Abraham did; his greatness is of a different order. Abraham was not only a great man of God, he was a great *man*. Some lives exhibit grand characteristics and yet there are curious defects; the only standard for judging the saint is Jesus Christ, not saintly qualities. Beware of the snare of taking people as types; no one is a type of anything; he may recall a particular type, but he is always something other than the type. If Abraham is taken as the type of a saint you get embarrassed because of the things in him which are not saintly. We are always inclined to remain true to our own ideas of a person; it does not matter what the facts are, we interpret all that he does according to our idea of him. If I accept you as an expression of my idea of you, I will be unjust to you as a fact; I make you either better or worse than you are, I never hit just 'you' until I learn to accept facts as facts.

## The Extraordinary Gentleness of Isaac

*(vv. 14–26)*

> Also Isaac's servants dug in the valley, and found a well of running [living] water there. But the herdsmen of Gerar quarrelled with Isaac's herdsmen saying, The water is ours. So he called the name of the well Esek [i.e., contention, RV marg.], because they quarrelled with him *(vv. 19–20)*.

The strife arose around a well of living water, and Isaac let them have it, that is, he refused to drink of the water of 'Contention'. Whenever a doctrinal well becomes 'Esek', give it up; your life with God is more precious than proving you are right doctrinally. It is at the peril of your communion with God that you contend about a doctrine. 'Then they dug another well, and they quarrelled over that one also' (v. 21). And Isaac surrendered it, calling it Sitnah, 'That is, Enmity' (RV marg.). It is a great sign of grace not to break your heart because you cannot drink of the water of 'Enmity'. 'And he moved from there and dug another well, and they did not quarrel over it. So he called its name Rehobeth, [i.e., Broad places or Room, RV marg.] because he said, For now the Lord has made room for us, and we shall be fruitful in the land' (v. 22).

'And the Lord appeared to him the same night and said, I am the God of your father Abraham; do not fear, for I am with you. I will bless you and multiply your descendants for my servant Abraham's sake' (v. 24). Isaac has come to a broad place and God appears to him, and for the first time the grand phrase, *'I am the God of Abraham'* appears. 'So he built an altar there, and called on the name of the Lord' (v. 25).

When you stand up for another who has been grossly wronged and your stand to be of any avail must have the co-operation of the wronged one, there is nothing more maddening than to find that he is without any resentment. That must have been the heartbreaking embarrassment to the disciples over our Lord; they had built up their own ideas as to how He was going to bring in His kingdom and they were prepared to fight for Him, then they saw Jesus meekly give Himself up to the power of the world. He did nothing whatever to assert His rights. In the Christian life the problem arises not from the world, which says you are a fool, but from your friends who are prepared to stand up for you.

Inoffensiveness, which is one of the chief characteristics of Isaac, usually means to our natural minds a quality unsuited to a strong personality. We have to bear in mind that the life of our Lord portrayed just this characteristic of inoffensiveness: 'He was led as a lamb to the slaughter, and as a sheep before its shearers is silent, so he opened not his mouth.' 'He was crucified through weakness,' and, 'we also are weak in Him.' Anything to do with meekness and submissiveness is antagonistic to robust human nature. Our impatience gets beyond its limit because of the characteristics Jesus Christ insists upon: *'Learn from me; for I am gentle and lowly in heart....'* The natural heart builds on adventure, recklessness, independence, impulse; the characteristics God prizes are produced only in the son of sacrifice. Natural inoffensiveness may be the weakness of constitutional timidity; supernatural inoffensiveness is almighty strength scorning to use the weapons of the flesh. Inoffensiveness is self-control indwelt by the Holy Spirit: 'the fruit of the Spirit is...self-control.'

### The Eternal and the Haphazard *(vv. 28–33)*

> Let there now be an oath between us, between you and us, and let us make a covenant with you.... So he made them a feast and they ate and drank. Then they arose early in the morning and swore an oath with one another.... It came to pass the same day that Isaac's servants came and told him about the well which they had dug, and said to him, We have found water. So he called it Shebah. Therefore the name of the city is Beersheba to this day [the well of the oath].

All the transactions entered into by both Abraham and Isaac, no matter how temporary or casual, were based on their relationship to God, that is, they used their wits in their worship of Him. This recognition of God began to be lost during Jacob's life, and the children of Israel went on ignoring it until they came to establish all their transactions on their own wits. Our Lord warns against taking an oath (see Matthew 5:33–35), because in the sight of God an oath means the recognition of God in the most temporary transaction. In the Old Testament, and in the record of the Resurrection, we find the temporary matter of eating and drinking put on the eternal foundation of relationship to God. The things which can be most easily ridiculed are the things that have most of God in them. A saint can be ridiculed because he sees haphazard happenings in the light of the eternal – 'The Lord guided me here, and there.' The fact that a man who is a fraud says the same thing as a saint is proof that he is counterfeiting something which is real. No actual fact has its right name unless you can worship God in it. Remember, whatever happens, God is there. It is easy to fix your mind on God in a lecture, but a different matter to fix your mind on Him when there is a war on. You never get at God by blinking facts, but only by naming Him in the facts; whether they are devilish or not, say, 'Lord, I thank you that you are here.'

FORTY-ONE

# PLANS AND PROVIDENCE

## *Chapter 27*

Now Rebekah was listening when Isaac spoke to Esau his son *(v. 5)*.

PLANS ARISE from the human 'must'—the imperative demand of my own undisciplined nature which makes me feel, 'I must do something; God is no use here.' God rarely rebukes us for our impulsive plans because those plans work their own distress. Plans made apart from trusting God's wisdom are rotten. *Providence* arises from God's majesty. The wisdom of God can never be according to man's understanding, and in our regenerated lives while we are 'climbing the slow ascensions' of our heavenly Father's wisdom, He engineers our circumstances by His providence and puts within our inmost soul the childlike joy of confidence in Himself. It is always easier not to trust; if I can work the thing out for myself then I am not going to trust in God. I work out a plan whereby I say God must do the thing and I force His hand along certain lines, and when He does what I said I knew He would do, for an exhilarating moment I think I have made Him do it! Then I find I am to be punished for everything I tried to make Him do, though it looks as if my wrong had brought about His good. Beware of egging God on; possess your soul in patience.

Always beware when you can reasonably account to yourself for the action you are about to take, because the source of such clear reasoning is the enthroning of human understanding. It is this element in the personal life of a Christian that fights longest and to the last against the enthronement of Jesus Christ as Lord and Master. 'Supposing I do say I will go to the foreign field, what about this, and that?' 'I want a reasonable explanation.' As long as you argue like that it is all up with devotion to Jesus Christ. He will have no influence over you until your plan is worked out because you have put your own wits on the throne. The reason we know so little about God's wisdom is that we will only trust Him as far as we can work things out according to our own reasonable common sense.

## Sensitiveness to Divinely Shaped Ends

*(vv. 6–17)*

> Now therefore, my son, obey my voice according to what I command you… *(vv. 8–17).*

Still waters run deep, but an able woman is deeper. Abraham made the supreme blunder of trying to help God fulfil His promise; Rebekah repeats the blunder. A woman with a sense of values in the end to be achieved cares nothing about herself in the accomplishing of that end. 'But his mother said to him, Let your curse be on me, my son; only obey my voice….' When a virtuous woman does wrong she does it with all the characteristic of her virtue transferred to the deception; Rebekah carried out her deception as though she were called and inspired of God to do it. In such a case the sin is not the outcome of impulse, but the deliberate perversion of integrity. In individual experience no one person is ever entirely to blame – 'my father is to blame, my mother, my heredity', everybody and everything but myself. It is impossible for human wisdom to apportion the blame. Remember the one fact more which God alone knows.

## SCHEMES OF DISCREET EXPECTATIONS *(vv. 18–25)*

> Then Rebekah took the choice clothes of her elder son Esau, which were with her in the house, and put them on Jacob her younger son... *(vv. 15–17).*

This is the first pious lie enacted in the Bible. Rebekah's motive was born of the oracles of God – '...and the older shall serve the younger' (25:23). Her act was entirely wrong; she enacted a lie in order to help God carry out His purpose. This is very different from the lie told for our own ends.

Jacob's enunciation of the lie – 'And Jacob said to his father, I am Esau your firstborn' is expressive fundamentally, not of self-seeking, but of devotion to his mother. Consequently, there is no hesitation or bravado because he is not yet so conscious as he will be of what he is doing. Beware of obeying anyone else's obedience to God because it means you are shirking responsibility yourself.

'Then his father Isaac said to him, Come near now, and kiss me, my son.... Be master over your brethren, and let your mother's sons bow down to you.' The whole lie is now enacted, and Jacob enters into the fullness of the blessing. God foreordained that the blessing should come to Jacob, but it was not part of that foreordination that Jacob should enter into the blessing in the way he did. There are experiences in human lives which are not part of God's purpose, but the result of human perversity. Remember, trust in

God does not mean that God will explain His solutions to us; it means that we are perfectly confident in God, and when we do see the solution we find it to be in accordance with all that Jesus Christ revealed of His character. It is nonsense to imagine that God expects me to discern all that is clear to His own mind; all He asks of me is to maintain perfect confidence in Himself. Faith springs from the indwelling of the life of God in me.

FORTY-TWO

# THE LONE QUEST

## *Chapter 28*

### THE DISCIPLINE OF THE UNCHANGING DESTINY
*(vv. 1–9)*

> May God Almighty bless you...that you may inherit the land in which you are a stranger, which God gave to Abraham *(vv. 3–4)*.

JACOB'S DESTINY had nothing to do with his personal character, but his personal character had everything to do with the desperate discipline he went through. God's destiny for a life will be fulfilled though the details of the fulfilment are determined by the individual. The kind of discipline Jacob went through was determined by his perversity. The 'lone quest' is never pathetic unless, as in Jacob's case, it is mixed with cunning and sin in motive.

'Was not Esau Jacob's brother? Says the Lord: yet Jacob I have loved, but Esau I have hated' (Mal. 1:2–3). In all implicit matters intuition is of more avail than logic. Naturally, we are inclined to love Esau and dislike Jacob. The most undesirable person in later life is often the one who was most desirable when young. A chaotic young life is always the most satisfactory. '...yet I have loved Jacob'—God loves the man who needs Him. Esau was satisfied with what he was; Jacob wanted more than he was. Esau never saw visions, never wrestled with angels, although God was as near to him as to Jacob. Esau refused to sacrifice anything to the spiritual; he could never think of anything but the present. He was willing to sell the promise of the future for a mess of pottage, and thereby he wronged himself far more than Jacob did.

### The Dream of the Unimagined Dignity *(vv. 10–22)*

> Then he dreamed, and behold, a ladder was set up on the earth, and its top reached to heaven; and there the angels of God were ascending and descending on it. And behold, the Lord stood above it ['beside him,' RV marg.] and said, I am the Lord God of Abraham your father and the God of Isaac; the land on which you lie I will give to you and your descendants. Also your descendants shall be as the dust of the earth; you shall spread abroad to the west and to the east, to the north and the south; and in you and in your seed all the families of the earth shall be blessed *(vv. 12–15).*

Jacob's dream was a vision of the purpose of God for all the families of the earth. The destiny of the people known as 'Israel' is forecast in this one lonely man. God did not *select* this people, He *elected* them. God created them from Abraham to be His servants until through them every nation came to know who Jehovah was. They mistook the election of God's purpose to be the election of God's favouritism, and the story of their distress is due to their determination to use themselves for purposes other than God's. To this day they survive miraculously; the reason for their survival is the purpose of God to be fulfilled through them. They can still wait, still see visions of God, and the time is coming when God's promise shall be fulfilled materialistically. The prophecies are frequently taken as pictures of spiritual blessings; they are much more than that.

'Then he dreamed, and behold a ladder was set up

on the earth, and its top reached to heaven.' The ladder symbolizes communication between God and man. The only Being in whom communication with God was never broken is the Lord Jesus Christ, and His claim is that through the Redemption He can put every one of us in the place where communication with God can be re-established. Paul's phrase 'in Christ' – the Mystical Christ, not the Historic Christ – is a revelation of the Redemption at work on our behalf. If I am 'in Christ' the angels of God are always ascending and descending on my behalf, and the voice that speaks is the voice of God (cf. John 1:51).

Beware of having a measuring-rod for the Almighty, of tying God up in His own laws. This pre-incarnate vision of God was given to such a man as Jacob was. It is dangerous to have the idea that we merit these things; immediately prayer or devotion is taken as the ground of God's blessing we are off the track. Prayer and devotion are simply the evidence that we are on God's plan; to be devoid of any sense of ill-being spiritually is a sign that we are not on God's plan. Jacob is the man who represents life as it is. The world is not made up of saints or of devils, but of people like you and me, and our real home is at the foot of the ladder with Jacob. Never say that God intends a man to have a domain of dreaming, mighty visions of God, and at the same time be dead towards God in his actual life. Jesus Christ claims that He can make the real and the actual one, as they were in His own life. When the vision comes it does not come to the 'Esau' type of man. He is so thick-hided that to talk to him about the nearness of God's presence is absurd; there is no meaning in it – that is absolutely true, there *is* no meaning in it, until he gets to the desolate spot. We cling to the certainty that the rational common-sense life is the right one; Jesus Christ stands for the fact that a life based on the Redemption is the only right one, consequently when a man shifts from the one to the other there is a period of desolation. Remember, there is a vast moral distance between Bethel and Peniel.

## The Dedication of the Unparalleled Dawn

*(vv. 16–20)*

> Then Jacob awoke from his sleep and said, Surely the Lord is in this place, and I did not know it. And he was afraid and said, How awesome is this place! This is none other than the house of God, and this is the gate of heaven! *(vv. 16–17).*

'This place' means just where it is not within the bounds of imagination to infer that God would be. 'And he called the name of that place Bethel ['The house of God', RV marg.] because there God was revealed unto him.' 'Every house of God is a gate of heaven where the impossible and the miraculous becomes the natural breath.' There is always an amazed surprise when we find what God brings with Him when He comes, He brings everything! (Jn 14:23).

It is in the dark night of the soul that the realization of God's presence breaks upon us: we never see God as long as, like Esau, we are perfectly satisfied with what we are. When 'I know that in me nothing good dwells', I begin to experience the miracle of seeing and hearing, not according to my senses, but according to the way the Holy Spirit interprets the word of God to me. Any number of people are happy without God, because happiness depends on not too profound an understanding of things; 'the god of this age has blinded their minds' ['thoughts', RV marg.] (2 Cor. 4:4). When the revelation of God's presence does come, it comes to those who are where Jacob was, in downright need and depression, knowing there is no help anywhere saving in God. As long as there is any vestige of human sufficiency it is all up with the message of God as far as we are concerned.

When we come to consider it, the phrase, 'the God of Jacob', is the greatest possible inspiration; it has in it the whole meaning of the gospel of Jesus Christ, who said, '...for I came not to call the righteous, but sinners.' Had we been left with such phrases as 'the God of Joseph', or 'the God of Daniel', it would have spelt hopeless despair for most of us; but 'the God of Jacob' means 'God is *my* God', the God not only of the noble character, but of the sneak. From the sneak to entire sanctification is the miracle of the grace of God.

FORTY-THREE

# LOVE

## *Chapter 29*

LOVE, MORE than any other experience in life, reveals the shallowness and the profundity, the hypocrisy and the nobility of human nature. In dealing with all implicit things, such as love, there is a danger of being sentimentally consistent to a doctrine or an idea while the actual life is ignored; we forget that we have to live in this world as human beings. Consistency in doctrine ought to work out into expression in actual life, otherwise it produces the humbug in us; we have the jargon of the real thing, but actually we are not there. Anything that makes a man keep up a posture is not real; e.g., it is not true to say that an understanding of the doctrine of sanctification will lead you into the experience; doctrinal exposition comes after the experience in order to bring the actual life into perfect harmony with the marvel of the work of God's grace.

### God and the Cult of the Passing Moment

> Then Jacob went on his journey, and came to the land of the people of the east... *(vv. 1–7).*

The true worship of God can only be maintained when the passing moments are seen as occurring in God's order. If you try to forecast the way God will work you will get into a muddle; live the life of a child and you will find that every haphazard occasion fits into God's order. 'The cult of the passing moment' means that you resolutely believe that 'all things work together for good to those who love God, to those who are the called according to his purpose'. Don't be your own god in these matters; be concentrated, not on the haphazard, but on God, who comes to you through the haphazard. Jacob is realizing God's order in the midst of the haphazard circumstances in which he finds himself; in the coming of Rachel he suddenly meets God.

## God and the Cult of the Passionate Moment

*(vv. 8–14)*

> Then Jacob kissed Rachel, and lifted up his voice, and wept *(v. 10).*

There is no safer guide in the matter of human love than the Bible, particularly the Old Testament. Solomon says a penetrating thing – 'I charge you ... do not stir up nor awaken love until it pleases' [before the time] (Song 2:7), and woe be to any such awakener. Many a man has awakened love before the time, and has reaped hell into the bargain. Love is awakened before the time whenever a man or woman ignores the worship of God and becomes a mere creature of impulsive passions. God cannot guard the natural heart that does not worship Him; it is at the mercy of every vagrant passion stirred by the nearness of another. Unless you are guided by God in your human relationships you will get a multitude of haphazard affairs that God is not in; there are the same haphazard affairs in the life of a child of God, but God is in them.

Beware of not worshipping God in your emotional

history. Watch your fancies and your friends, heed who you love and who loves you, and you will be saved from many a pitfall.

## God and the Cult of the Parenthetic Moment

*(vv. 15–20)*

> Now Jacob loved Rachel; and he said, I will serve you seven years for Rachel *(v. 18).*

Jacob was what he was – mean, yet in the most mixed human life there may come a parenthesis which is pure and unsullied. Mark well the parentheses God puts into your human life. There is not a passage in the whole of the Bible to equal verse 20 for a description of pure human love: 'So Jacob served seven years for Rachel, and they seemed but a few days to him because of the love he had for her.' Sacrifice for love is never conscious; sacrifice for duty always has margins of distress. The nature of love is to give, not to receive. Talk to a lover about giving up anything, and he doesn't begin to understand you!

Love is not blind; love sees a great deal more than the actual – it sees the ideal in the actual, consequently the actual is transfigured by the ideal. That is a different thing from 'halo-slinging', which means you have your own idea about other people and expect them to live up to it, and then when they don't, you blame them. An ideal is not a halo; it is reality made clear to you by intuition. If you love someone you are not blind to his defects but you see the ideal which exactly fits that one. God sees all our crudities and defects, but He also sees the ideal for us; He sees 'every man perfect in Christ Jesus', consequently He is infinitely patient.

## God and the Cult of the Paralleled Measure

*(vv. 25–30)*

> What is this you have done to me? Was it not for Rachel that I served you? Why then have you deceived me? *(v. 25).*

The humour of God is sometimes tragic; He engineers across our path the kind of people who exhibit to us our own characteristics – not very flattering, is it? In this chapter we see the beguiler beguiled; Jacob was deceived, but he also was a deceiver. We say, 'I wonder why this should happen to me?' Remember the Apostle Paul's words: 'But he who does wrong will be repaid for the wrong which he has done, and there is no partiality' (Col. 3:25).

FORTY-FOUR

# DEGENERATION

*Chapters 29 — 30*

DEGENERATION AND backsliding are by no means one and the same. Degeneration begins in almost imperceptible ways; backsliding in the scriptural use of the term is a distinct forsaking of what I know of God and a deliberate substitution of something other (cf. Jeremiah 2:13).

A point on which we need to be alert is that the presence of the life of the Son of God in us does not alter our human nature; God does remove the disposition of sin, but He demands of us that our human nature 'puts on the new man', and no longer fashions itself according to its former natural desires. This is what the Apostle Paul means by his use of the term 'mortify' (Col. 3:5), viz., destroy by neglect. The spiritual application is that the natural must be sacrificed in order that it may be turned into the spiritual. This law works all through. Esau stands for the natural life refusing to obey. If I maintain my right to my natural self I will begin to degenerate and get out of God's purpose. What happens in my personal life when I am born from above is that the Son of God is born in me; then comes in this law of the sacrifice of the natural to the spiritual, and the possibility of degeneration. If I refuse to sacrifice the natural, the God-life in me is killed.

## When the Reward of Sin is More Sinfulness

Chapter 29 records the retribution Jacob experienced for his own deceitfulness – Jacob impersonates Esau; Laban makes Leah impersonate Rachel. Beware what you permit in your relationships because you will 'be-done-by-as-you-did', and the reason for it is God. The inexorable law is stated in Matthew 7 – 'For with what judgment you judge you will be judged; and with the same measure you use, it will be measured back to you.' The wrong began with Abraham and Hagar, and it works straight through 'the maddening maze of things'; the only line of extrication is through the Redemption. It is one thing to deceive other people, but you have to get up very early if you want to take in God!

## Where the Ruin of Sanctity is Mixed Sanctity

*(30:1–24)*

Jacob's home becomes a place of friction – no man ever gave his heart to two women – yet gleams of joy come to it. Every child is regarded by the Hebrew as a gift of God, and the naming of Jacob's children reveals how closely men felt God to be bound up with their history.

If you indulge in practices which the Holy Spirit condemns, or in imaginations you have no business to indulge in, the appalling lash of ruined sanctity is that 'my sin finds *me* out'. 'If I could only fling the whole thing overboard!' – but you cannot. God has made the way of transgressors hell on earth. The first mark of degeneration is to deem a wrong state permissible, and then propose it as a condition of sanctity. We only turn in disgust from the details in God's Book when we forget who we are. Nothing has ever been done by human nature that any member of the human family may not be trapped into doing; the only safeguard is to keep in the light as God is in the light.

### WHERE RETRIBUTION OF SELFISHNESS TURNS TO SPITE *(vv. 25–43)*

Jacob has been robbed, and now he retaliates; his aim is to enrich himself at Laban's expense and he succeeds absolutely – 'Thus the man became exceedingly prosperous, and had large flocks, female and male servants, and camels and donkeys' (v. 43).

Beware of the inspiration that springs from impulse, because impulse enthrones self-lordship as God. My impulses can never be disciplined by anyone saving myself, not even by God. If my impulses are domineered over by somebody else, that one will find sooner or later that he or she has sat on a safety valve – always a risky thing to do. Unless I discipline my impulses they will ruin me, no matter how generous they may be. The revelation to ourselves in studying other people's lives ought to make us eager to realize that 'no good thing dwells in me'.

FORTY-FIVE

# THE CRISIS IN CIRCUMSTANCES

## *Chapter 31*

Then the Lord said to Jacob, Return to the land of your fathers *(v. 3).*

NO MAN'S destiny is made for him; each man makes his own. Fatalism is the deification of moral cowardice which arises from a refusal to accept the responsibility for choosing either of the two destined ends for the human race—salvation or damnation. The power of individual choice is the secret of human responsibility. I can choose which line I will go on, but I have no power to alter the destination of that line once I have taken it—yet I always have the power to get off one line on to the other.

### CONFUSION IN CONSECRATION *(vv. 4–10)*

Jacob would seem to think that to do things openly when you might do them obscurely is a sign of feeble intelligence; all his outwitting has not taught him wisdom. The apparent piece of humbug which these verses record is not really humbug at all; it is a repetition of what happened in the matter of the birthright, in which Isaac and Rebekah, Jacob and Esau, all did wrong, and yet out of it came the fulfilment of God's purpose. The blunder lies in trying to help God fulfil

His own word. God's word will be fulfilled, but if I reach its fulfilment through committing sin, God must crush me in chastisement; the chastisement has no part in His order; it comes in under His permissive will.

### Call to Conscience *(vv. 11–13)*

Jacob has brought back to him his dream at Bethel when God appeared to him and spoke to him — 'I am the God of Bethel where you anointed the pillar and where you made a vow to me. Now arise, get out of this land, and return to the land of your kindred.' Jacob's character exhibits human nature as it is better than any other Bible character — the high mountain peaks and the cesspools, they all come out. No man is so bad but that he is good enough to know he is bad. Beware of insisting on attainments which are impossible to human nature before the possibilities of the divine nature have come in — demanding of human nature that it should be what it never can be. Jesus Christ died for the *ungodly*, for the *weak*, for *sinners*; if we put the fruits of the Redemption as the reason for God's forgiveness, we belittle His salvation. God's call comes, not to human nature, but to conscience, and when a man obeys what God reveals to a thoroughly awakened conscience, then begins the possibility in human nature of the expression of the life of God. To experience conviction of sin is not a cause for misgiving, but an occasion for understanding the impossible thing God has done in the Redemption.

### Calamity in Estrangement *(vv. 14–35)*

So he fled with all that he had.... *(v. 21).*

Jacob's flight and its attendant perplexities is the best unveiling of the unutterable muddle the most acute human wisdom can get into, and serves as another indication of the truth of the revelation that 'A man's goings are of the Lord; how then can man understand his way?' Crises reveal that we don't believe this; the only God we worship is our own wits. All through, a personal crisis ought to serve as an occasion for revealing the fact that God reigns, as well as compelling us to know our own character. You may think yourself to be generous and noble until a crisis comes, and you suddenly find you are a cad and a coward; no one else finds it out, but you do. To be found out by yourself is a terrible thing.

'Now Rachel had taken the household idols...' (v. 34). In the centre of the family is Rachel, and she outwits Laban and Jacob by stealing the household gods. 'And Rachel had stolen the household idols that were her fathers' (v. 19). There are only two beings a woman is not too much for: one is God, the other is the devil. A mascot is a talisman of some sort the presence of which is supposed to bring good luck. The persistence of the superstitious element is one of the most indelible stains on the character of otherwise good people, and it abounds in our own day. A reawakening of superstition always follows on the heels of gross materalism in personal and in national life. When once the 'mascot' tendency is allowed in the temple of the Holy Spirit, spiritual muddle-headedness is sure to result. Beware of excusing spiritual muddle-headedness in yourself; if it is not produced by the 'Jacob' reserve, it is produced by the 'Rachel' wit, and the only way out of the muddle is to walk in the light.

FORTY-SIX

# MAHANAIM

## *Chapter 32*

OF ALL THE Bible characters Jacob ever remains the best example of the recipient of God's life and power, simply because of the appalling mixture of the good and the bad, the noble and the ignoble in him. His nobility is never far to seek in the midst of it all. We have the notion that it is only when we are pure and holy that God will appear to us; that God's blessing is a sign that we are right with Him. Neither notion is true. Our Lord took care to say that 'God makes his sun to rise on the evil and on the good, and sends his rain on the just and on the unjust'. God's blessings are not to be taken as an indication of the integrity of the character blessed, yet on the other hand the discernment of God's character is determined entirely by the individual character of the person estimating God. 'With the merciful you will show yourself' (Ps. 18:24–26). The way I will discern God's character is determined by my own character. God remains true to His character, and as I grow in integrity I discern Him. Jacob's undeservedness, and the fact that God continually blesses him, are brought out very clearly all through his life.

### THE VENTURE OF THE MISGIVING WAY

And Jacob went on his way.

A sense of personal unworthiness is frequently the reaction of overweening conceit; genuine unworthiness has no conscious interest in itself. A genuinely unworthy nature is always possessed of sufficient nobility to face the inevitable – 'So Jacob went on his way'; that is the noble streak. The study of Jacob under the light of the Spirit of God is not exhilarating, but it is a wholesome cure for spiritual swagger. Whenever you get a real dose of your own unworthiness you are never conscious of it because you are so certain you are unworthy that you have the courage of despair. The first thing the Spirit of God does when He comes in is to bring this sense of unworthiness. Most of us suspend judgement about ourselves; we find reasons for not accusing ourselves entirely, consequently when we find anything so definite and intense as the Bible revelation we are apt to say it exaggerates, until we are smitten with the knowledge of what we are like in God's sight. If you can come to God without a feeling of your own contemptibility it is questionable whether you have ever come. The most humiliating thing in self-examination is that the passion of indignation we indulge in regarding others is the measure of our self-detection (see Romans 2:1).

## The Vision of the Ministering Witnesses

and the angels of God met him *(v. 1)*.

Isn't that indiscreet of God! The appearances of God are not so much a testimony to the goodness of the individual as the revelation of God Himself. Every estimate of God must be brought to the standard of the revelation made of Him by our Lord. The appearance of the angels of God is apt to be looked upon as the result of disordered nerves; but it is only when external conditions are hopeless to the human outlook that we are in a fit state to perceive the revelation. We are content where we are as long as things have not got to the hopeless condition, and when we do get there we are sentimentally interested in our own pathos—'Whatever shall I do when this, or that, happens?' When it does happen, you will see the angels of God. There is no such thing as dull despair anywhere in the Bible; there is tragedy of the most appalling order, but an equally amazing hopefulness—always a door deeper down than hell which opens into heaven.

## The Voice of the Mastering Wonder

> When Jacob saw them, he said, This is God's camp. And he called the name of that place Mahanaim ['double camp'] *(v. 2)*.

The sight of the two companies (camps), the earthly and the heavenly, is a fitting revelation of God's rule and government in this order of things. The reason so few of us see the hosts of God is that we have never let go of things as they are, never let go of our small parochial notions, of the sense of our own whiteness and respectability, consequently there is no room for God at all. Beware of the abortion of God's grace which prostitutes the Holy Spirit to the personal private use of my own whiteness, instead of allowing God by His majestic grace to keep me loyal to His character in spite of everything that transpires. Faith in God does not mean that He presents me as a museum specimen, but it does mean that however ignoble I may feel, I remain true to God's character no matter what perplexities may rage.

God's angelic hosts are like His visible mercies,

countless. We are economically drunk nowadays; everybody is an economist, consequently we imagine that God is economical. Think of God in creation! Think of the number of trees and blades of grass and flowers, the extravagant wealth of beauty no one ever sees! Think of the sunrises and sunsets we never look at! God is lavish in every degree. For God's sake, don't be economical; be God's child.

FORTY-SEVEN

# MISGIVING

## *Chapter 32:3–21*

MISGIVING IS the pathetic poem of the whole of human life in a word; it signifies the destruction of confidence. Many things will destroy confidence. As in the case of Jacob, cunning and sin will do it, or cowardice; but in every experience of misgiving there is an element which it is difficult to define, and the shallow element is the most difficult. 'I can't understand why I have no confidence in God'; the reason may be a matter of digestion; not enough fresh air, or sleep, too much tea – something slight. It is the shallow things that put us wrong much more quickly than the big things. The great object of the enemy of our souls is to make us fling away our confidence in God; to do this is nothing less than spiritual suicide. When we experience misgiving because we have sinned there is never any ambiguity as to its cause; the Holy Spirit brings conviction home like a lightning flash.

### THE APPOINTMENT OF THE MESSENGERS *(vv. 3–5)*

> Then Jacob sent messengers before him to Esau his brother... *(v. 3).*

Jacob has had a vision of God's power, but now he begins to put prudent methods on foot in case God should be obliged to let him down on account of his cunning. We have all got 'Uriah Heep' tucked away somewhere; his original form is found in Jacob. Every one of us has the possibility of every type of meanness any human being has ever exhibited; not to believe this is to live in a fool's paradise.

### The Apprehension of the Manoeuvres *(vv. 6–8)*

So Jacob was greatly afraid and distressed *(v. 7)*.

Jacob has still no intention of confessing his wrong, and his apprehensiveness on this account leads him to manoeuvre. Beware of the 'yes-but', of putting your prudence-crutch under the purpose of God when you find His engineering of things has nearly unearthed your own little bag of tricks. Whenever you debate with a promise of God, watch how you begin to manoeuvre by your own prudence – but you can't sleep at night. Whenever you manoeuvre it keeps up a ferment because it indicates a determination not to confess where you know you are wrong, and when we experience misgiving on account of wrongdoing which we do not intend to confess we are always inclined to put a crutch under God's promise – 'Now I see how I can make atonement for my wrongdoing.' Nothing can act as an atonement for wrong saving an absolutely clean confession to God. To walk in the light with nothing folded up is our conscientious part, then God will do the rest.

### The Appeal of Misgiving *(vv. 9–12)*

Deliver me I pray, from the hand of my brother, from the hand of Esau: for I fear him... *(v. 11)*.

Prayer in distress dredges the soul (cf. Psalm 107). It is a good thing to keep a note of the things you prayed about when you were in distress. We remain ignorant of ourselves because we do not keep a spiritual autobiography. Jacob's misgivings while in the attitude of prayer arise from the fact that while there is that in him which causes him to obey God, he is apprehensive lest God should punish him for his wrongdoing; he has to come to the place where he willingly confesses his guilt before God. Remember, Jacob did not turn back; he was cunning and crafty, but he was not a coward. There was not a strand of the physical coward in Jacob, but he was a moral coward by reason of his guilty conscience. His misgivings arose from his misdeeds.

Beware of having plans in your petitions before God; they are the most fruitful source of misgiving. If you pray along the line of your plans misgivings are sure to come, and if the misgivings are not heeded you will pervert God's purpose in the very thing which was begun at His bidding. God begins a work by the inspiration of the Holy Spirit for His own ends entirely and we get caught up into His purpose for that thing; then we begin to introduce our own plans – 'I want *this* to produce *that*,' and we storm the throne of God along that line. The first thing God does is *not* to do it, and we say, 'That must be the devil.' Beware of making God an item, even the principal item, in your programme. God's ways are curiously abrupt with programmes; He seems to delight in breaking them up.

## The Atonement for Misdeeds *(vv. 13–21)*

> So he lodged there that same night, and took what came to his hand as a present for Esau his brother *(v. 13)*.

Watch your motive for giving presents; it is a good way of discerning what a mean sneak you are capable of being. The giving of presents is one of the touchstones of character. If your relationship with God is not right in your present-giving, you will find there is an abomination of self-interest in it somewhere, even though you do it out of a warm-hearted impulse; there is a serpent-insinuation in it. It creeps into all our charity unless the life is right with God.

The cunning way in which the present is made to Esau is obvious, and yet Jacob is getting near the place where 'Peniel' is possible. Restitution in some form or other is as certain as that God is on His throne. Restitution on the human plane is the evidence that it was God who designed human nature. Watch the almost uncanny accuracy with which the Holy Spirit will bring a thing back – 'Therefore if you bring your gift to the altar, and there remember that your brother has something against you,' the Spirit of God brings it to you direct, '...go your way; first be reconciled to your brother.' Beware how you deal with yourself when God is educating you down to the scruple; it is nearly always some ridiculously small thing that keeps you from getting through to God. Human nature looks for something big, yet it is some little thing; but behind it is the disposition of my prideful right to myself. 'First go...'.

FORTY-EIGHT

# PENIEL

*Chapter 32:22–32*

PENIEL MEANS 'face of God', and the word to Moses stands – 'But He said, You cannot see my face: for no man shall see me and live' (Ex. 33:20). This gives peculiar force to Jacob's words, 'I have seen God face to face, and my life is preserved', for Jacob did see God face to face, and he did die, so profound a death that God gave him a new name. 'Your name shall no longer be called Jacob, but Israel.' That is always the test of the reality of sanctification, not so much that I have received something, but that I have ceased to be my old self. Through disillusionment and shattering Jacob comes out on God's side with a changed name; we drag the purpose of God through our own plans and change His name. We have to learn to distinguish between the impression made on us by a vision, and identification with the One who gave us the vision. The love of God and His forgiveness are the first things we experience; we are not prepared as yet to recognize His other attributes of holiness and justice because that will mean death to everything that does not partake of God's nature.

## The Struggle of Anguish

Then Jacob was left alone *(v. 24)*.

This phrase is significant because in his loneliness Jacob goes through the decisive struggle of his life. We are dealing in this chapter with Jacob the giant, not with the mean man. '...and a man wrestled with him until the breaking of day.' Jacob tried to strangle the answer to his own prayer; his wrestling represents the human fighting with God. The nobler ones in God's sight are those who do not struggle but go through without demur. Abraham did not wrestle, neither did Isaac; Jacob struggles for everything. If a man has difficulty in getting through to God we are apt to imagine it is an indication of a fine character, whereas the opposite is true; he is refusing to yield and is kicking, and the only thing God can do is to cripple him. The characteristics exhibited by Jacob are those of Peter before Pentecost, of Saul of Tarsus before his conversion—a mixture of the dastardly and the heroic, the mean and the noble, all jumbled up. Jacob's wrestling is a profounder thing than the meeting with his brother; there is not one word about Esau in all that follows. Jacob is face to face with his need to acknowledge God and be blessed by Him.

## The Surrender of All

I will not let you go, unless you bless me *(v. 26).*

This is the picture of Jacob's full renunciation. When the supreme crisis is reached in a mixed soul like Jacob something must die, either self-realization or God. To the simpler nature the crisis need not come at all, but to the mean, the ambitious, and the proud, it must come, and God does not show Himself as gentleness, but as adamant. It means death without the slightest hope of resurrection. What it is that goes to death depends on me. Am I willing to let the wrong in me that cannot dwell with God go to death, or willing to let the life of God die out in me? The crisis may be reached in an apparently placid commonplace life; there may be no external sign of it, but there is an internal crumbling away from all that is pure and holy. Jacob was not like that; he did not refuse to go through the inward struggle of his own nature against the blazing holiness of God.

## The Solicitation of Appeal

> So he said to him, What is your name? And he said, Jacob *(v. 27).*

The confession has to be made: That is my name — supplanter; sneak; there is no palliation. Jacob had to get to the place where he willingly confesses before God the whole guilt of usurping the birthright. This is full and profound and agonizing repentance. 'And he said, Your name shall no longer be called Jacob, but Israel; for you have struggled with God and with men, and have prevailed.' The warrior of God is not the man of muscle and a strong jaw, but the man of unutterable weakness, the man who knows he has not any power. Jacob is no longer strong in himself; he is strong only in God. His life is no longer marked by striving, but by reliance on God. You cannot imitate reliance on God.

> Not by wrestling, but by clinging
> Shall we be most blest;
>
> Unconditional surrender
> Brings us God's own peace.

Jacob's wrestling means that he did not want to go through the way he knew he must; he had to come to the end of the best of his natural self, and he struggled in order not to. Then he came to the place where his wisdom was crippled for ever: 'and he limped on his hip.' The symbol is expressive of what it looks like in the eyes of shrewd worldly wisdom to cast yourself unperplexed on God. When we cling to God we learn to kneel for the first time.

If you have never been to 'Peniel' you are sure to come across things that will put your human wisdom into a panic; if you have seen God face to face your circumstances will never arouse any panic in you. We run off at a tangent – anywhere but Peniel, where we would see God 'face to face'.

FORTY-NINE

# THE STILL SMALL VOICE

*Chapters 33 — 35*

ON THE SURFACE everything seemed right enough to Jacob in Shechem, but underneath the surface everything was wrong. Everything is always wrong when the children of God dwell in Shechem instead of at Bethel. This chapter is the unveiling by God of the actuality of sin.

'Then Jacob came safely to the city of Shechem' (v. 18). One day the hollow 'Shechem' peace was shaken by an earthquake—Dinah's fall, and her brothers' crime, rudely awakened Jacob; then God's voice was heard: 'Arise, go up to Bethel, and dwell there.'

To enter into peace for ourselves without becoming either tolerantly unwatchful of other lives or an amateur providence over them, is supremely difficult. God holds us responsible for two things in connection with the lives He brings around us in the apparent haphazard of His providence, viz., insistent waiting on God for them, and inspired instruction and warning from God to them. The thing that astonishes us when we get through to God is the way God holds us responsible for other lives.

## THE AWAKENING VOICE OF GOD

Then God said to Jacob, Arise, go up to Bethel, and dwell there... *(35:1)*.

This must be the voice of God; no human voice would ever have said what these words imply. Think what Bethel meant to Jacob in memory—Bethel was the geographical place of God to him: 'How awesome is this place! This is none other than the house of God, and this is the gate of heaven.' Bethel was the place where the divine promises had been given, and vows made, not yet fulfilled. To go back to Bethel meant to acknowledge error. The voice of God to an awakened soul, when it has heard the voice before, is never to go forward, but to go back. When the blood runs high and impulse worships at the shrine of the heroic, and the nerves strain for the actual doing of something, we not only do not hear God's voice, we don't want to hear it. Then when events have produced an earthquake in the personal life, we find that God was not in the earthquake, but in the still small voice, 'Go to Bethel, and stay there.'

### The Arousing Virtue of God *(vv. 2–4)*

> And Jacob said to his household and to all who were with him, Put away the foreign gods that are among you... *(v. 2).*

Now that Jacob has heard the voice of God speaking to him he is not afraid to assert his authority in his household. When you come across a man or woman who talks to you from God, you know it by the intuition of your spirit and you obey him, scarcely realizing what you are doing; on looking back you become aware that it was not a human voice at all but the voice of God. Simulated authority should be laughed at, and it is a downright sensible human duty to do so; but when the authority of God comes to you through anyone, to rebel against it would be to rebel against

God. But beware of trying to be consistent to the authority that God gives you over any life on a particular occasion; you know that God used you then in that life and you say, 'Now I am always going to have this authority' – that is wrong. Authority never comes from you, but from God through you, therefore let God introduce or withhold as He chooses.

## The Appreciated Value of God

> Then let us arise, and go up to Bethel; and I will make an altar to God there... *(v. 3).*

Every expansion of heart or brain or spirit must be paid for in added concentration. In the meeting with Esau and the marvellous experience of reconciliation with him, Jacob had an expansion of heart, but he did not pay for it afterwards in concentration; he lived loosely in the exalted peace of the expanded life, and suddenly a terrible tragedy breaks up the whole thing. In our personal lives every expansion of heart, whether it is the awakening of human love, or bereavement, must be paid for by watchfulness; if it is not, looseness, the feeling of all-abroadness, ending in moral collapse, is sure to result. It is because people do not understand the way they are made that all the havoc is produced in the lives of those who really have had times with God and experienced expansions of heart, but they have forgotten to concentrate, and the general feeling of looseness is a sure sign that God's presence has gone.

'Who answered me in the day of my distress, and has been with me in the way which I have gone' – the implication is, 'when God answered me and brought deliverance, I forgot all about Him.' Jacob settled down in the peace of Shechem, Dinah went to hell, and her brothers to the devil; then God spoke to Jacob. If you allow your mind to be expanded and forget to concentrate on God, the thing that happened in Jacob's domestic life on the big scale will happen in your bodily life on the narrow scale. The vision of what God wants must be paid for by concentration on your part; if it is not, you begin to get all abroad, and in come the 'little foxes', in comes inordinate affection, in comes a hundred and one things that were never there before, and down you go. It is not that these things may happen; they *will* happen as sure as God is God, unless you watch and pray, that is, concentrate until you are confirmed in the ways of God.

Innocence must be transfigured into virtue by moral choices. We are all apt to be taken in by a frank nature. The man we call frank says of a wrong thing, 'I'm sorry I did it', and promptly does it again, and we forgive him, while all the time the deepest devilry goes on. The frank nature brings the glamour of virtue without its reality and stings innocence to death. Innocence is not purity; innocence is right for a child, but criminal for a man or woman. Men and women have no business to be innocent; they ought to be virtuous and pure. Character must be attained.

Individuality, impulse, and innocence are the husk of personal life. Individuality, if it goes beyond a certain point, becomes pig-headedness, determined independence. I have to be prepared to give up my independent right to myself in order that my personality may emerge. Impulse is a subtle snare, always and every time; it may start right, but it is a short-cut to fame or infamy, and it is along the line of impulse that lust and temptation comes. Hold back the impulse and you discipline it into character, and it becomes something altogether different, viz., intuition. The same thing with innocence; innocence must be transformed into purity by a series of moral choices. There is no virtue that has not gone through a moral choice. A great many of us make virtues out of necessity.

FIFTY

# THE BOY OF GOD

## *Chapters 37 — 50*

### Ideals of Seventeen

Joseph, being seventeen years old... *(37:2).*

The Bible always incarnates ideals in great personalities, and Joseph stands for the magnificent integrity of boyhood; no man thinks so clearly or has such high ideals as in his teens, but unless our ideals find us living in accordance with them they become a mockery. The Bible pays no attention to intellectual and emotional conceptions, but only to the actual manifestation of the ideal. A man may have remarkable conceptions, fine intellectual views, noble ideals and his actual life be beneath contempt, proving that all the high ideals and intellectual conceptions in the world have not the slightest power to bring the life into contact with Reality. There is no room whatever in our Lord's teaching for ideals and a stumbling walk of the feet; there must be an at-one-ment between the God-inspired conceptions and actual life, and the only way this can be brought about is by 'coming to me'.

Joseph was amazingly susceptible to God, and he 'dreamed dreams' (see vv. 5, 9). The dreams of the Old Testament are the touch of God on the spirit of a man; always reverence such dreams. 'And they hated him even more for his dreams, and for his words' (v. 8). The hatred produced by a sense of superiority in another is the most venomous. This gives the inner meaning of our Lord's words: 'They hated me without a cause.' Beware what you brood on in secret for the fateful opportunity will come when God and the devil will meet in your soul, and you will do according to your brooding, swept beynd all your control. This is a law as sure as God is God. The fateful opportunity came to the brethren who hated Joseph – 'Now when they saw him afar off, even before he came near them, they conspired against him to kill him.' Beware of saying, 'Oh well, it doesn't matter much what I think about in secret'; it does, for the opportunity will come when what you think about in secret will find expression and spurt out in an act. The Bible always speaks of sin as it appears in its final analysis. Jesus does not say, 'You must not covet because it will lead to stealing'; He says, 'You must not covet because it *is* stealing.' He does not say, 'You must not be angry with your brother because it will lead to murder'; He says, 'You must not be angry with your brother because it *is* murder.' 'Whoever hates his brother is a murderer' (1 Jn 3:15). When the climax of these things is reached we begin to see the meaning of Calvary.

## 'His Strength was as the Strength of Ten'

> The Lord was with Joseph, and he was a successful man; and he was in the house of his master the Egyptian *(39:2)*.

A life with presence, i.e., an uncommon spirit, redeems any situation from the commonplace. It may be cleaning boots, doing housework, walking in the street, any ordinary thing at all, but immediately it is touched by a man or woman with presence it ceases to be commonplace. The rarest asset to a godly life is to be practically conscientious in every situation. 'But the Lord was with Joseph...and gave him favour in the sight of the keeper of the prison' (v. 21). Joseph's adaptability was superb. Adaptability is not tact—tact is frequently nothing but the moral counterpart of hypocrisy. Adaptability is the power to make a suitable environment for oneself out of any set of circumstances. Most of us are all right if we can live in our own particular setting, with our own crowd, but when we get pitchforked somewhere else either we cannot adapt ourselves, or we adapt ourselves too easily and lose God. Joseph did not lose God; God was with Joseph in Egypt as in Canaan, with him in the prison as in the house of his master. If I simply delight in a godly atmosphere and refuse to appropriate God for myself, when I have to leave the godly atmosphere I will find myself God-less; then my natural adaptability becomes the adaptability to degenerate.

## 'Complete Steel'

> ...How then can I do this great wickedness, and sin against God? *(39:9).*

The phrase 'complete steel' is Milton's definition of chastity, and is peculiarly appropriate to Joseph. Personal chastity is an impregnable barrier against evil. Like virtue, chastity is not a gift, but an attainment of determined integrity. Unsoiledness may be nothing more than necessity, the result of a shielded life, and is no more chastity than innocence is purity. Virtue and chastity are forged by me, not by God. You can't drown a cork, and you can't defile Joseph.

Four times over in this chapter is the statement

made, 'the Lord was with Joseph.' It is the presence of God that is the secret of victory always. The fear of the Lord creates an atmosphere in which impure thoughts and unholy desires die a natural death. 'But I did not do so, because of the fear of God' (see Nehemiah 5:15). Joseph knew that the God whom he worshipped was 'of purer eyes than to behold evil, and could not look on iniquity'. The outstanding value of the Bible is that it makes shameful things appear shameful because it never analyses them.

The discovery of the desperate recesses in the human heart is the greatest evidence of the need for the Redemption. The experiences of life awaken possibilities of evil that make you shudder, and as long as we remain under the refuge of innocence we are fools. The appalling things revealed in human lives confirm the words of the great Master of the human heart. Our Lord did not say, *'into the heart of man* "these things" *are injected'*, but, *'from within, out of the heart of man, proceed...'* and then follows the terrible catalogue. We ought to get into the habit of estimating ourselves by this rugged standard. The important thing to remember is that we are better trusting the revelations of Jesus Christ than our own innocence. The only thing that safeguards is the Redemption.

> And God sent me before you to preserve a posterity [remnant] for you in the earth, and to save your lives by a great deliverance *(45:7)*.

That was Joseph's high vocation, to preserve life. God brings His purposes to pass in spite of all men may do, and often through what they do, and He will utilize the very things which look as if they were going dead against their fulfilment; God goes steadily on and involves us in the fulfilment.

So now it was not you who sent me here, but God *(45:8)*.

But as for you, you meant evil against me, but God meant it for good *(50:20)*.